JURY TRIALS CLASSROOM

Written by: **Betty M. See**

Legal Advisor: **Diane Elizabeth See**

Illustrated by: **Stephanie OíShaughnessy**

First published in 2006 by Prufrock Press Inc.

Published in 2021 by Routledge
605 Third Avenue, New York, NY 10017
2 Park Square, Milton Park, Abingdon, Oxon OX14 4RN

Routledge is an imprint of the Taylor & Francis Group, an informa business

ISBN: 9781032142531 (hbk)
ISBN: 9781593630850 (pbk)

DOI: 10.4324/9781003236092

Contents

Acknowledgments

Chief Nelson Romaine of the Little Falls, New Jersey, Police Department was instrumental in turning our mock trials from a classroom exercise into an activity that was extremely realistic. For many years, he arranged for the use of the Little Falls Municipal Courtroom and contacted local and county judges to preside at our trials.

The "Rules of Evidence and Procedure" included in Chapter 4 were derived from the "Simplified Rules of Evidence and Procedure" of the 1992 Statewide Mock Trial Tournament Materials, from the New York State Bar Association. They are reprinted here with the permission from the New Jersey State Bar Association and the New York State Bar Association.

Introduction

Jury Trials and the Middle School Curriculum

Teachers are always looking for activities that will not only challenge their students intellectually but also ignite enthusiasm for learning. They seek for their classrooms the magical combination of being able to introduce relevant new information or skills in a venue that captures students' interest. Doing mock trails is such an activity. Relevant, challenging, motivating, and engaging, it will become one of your favorite classroom adventures.

Mock trials present students with situations (usually fictional in nature) where the parties involved could have had their differences resolved in a courtroom. Students then take on the roles of attorneys, defendants, plaintiffs, witnesses, and jurors. In a classroom courtroom they prepare arguments to support each side and in the end resolve the issue by a vote of the jury.

This activity accomplishes several objectives at the same time. Mock jury trials provide opportunities for students to:
- understand the judicial system
- work cooperatively
- write persuasive statements
- read analytically
- integrate information from several sources
- think evaluatively and render judgments
- prepare and deliver oral presentations

How Jury Trials was Developed

When I first started working with gifted students in Little Falls, New Jersey, I knew that the biggest challenge would be to provide them with activities that were interesting and allowed them to explore different viewpoints.

My first attempts at conducting mock trials in the classroom were based on materials supplied by the local bar association. Students were divided into two teams, one representing the prosecution or plaintiff and the other representing the defense. We held trials in front of an audience and used members of the audience as jurors.

The trials were an immediate success, and the students eagerly looked forward to their turns to participate in an activity that was so realistic. As we looked for new trials, we found that the trials that were supplied by the bar association were not always suitable for students in grades five through eight. The solution was to write original trials. Thus, began the process that resulted in this book, *Jury Trials in the Classroom*.

Starting with the case of Jack and Jill, I developed a scenario and began writing believable, balanced affidavits for each character. When that case was successfully resolved, I worked with my classes to develop, test, and refine five other trials, some based on fairy tales or literature and one based on a historical event (the murder of President Lincoln).

I was fortunate at each step to have my daughter Diane, a criminal defense attorney, as a reference resource. She gave me advice on the legal aspects of each case that added to the validity of each case.

Grade Level Recommendations

In my experience, I have found that students in grades five and six tend to enjoy the trials based on children's stories more than older students. Although it is possible to use these trials with older groups, the trials based on Lincoln's assassination and the story of Romeo and Juliet have a higher interest value for them. The Booth trial can easily be used as part of a memorable U.S. history lesson, and the trial of *Lord Capulet v. Friar Laurence* lends itself beautifully to the multi-disciplinary approach of a social studies and literature activity. The trials that are presented in this book will give students opportunities to view familiar stories from different points of view.

A Great Adventure Awaits

With the materials in this book, you have the resources to produce six mock trials. These trials will be one of your students' most memorable educational endeavors. A mock trial is a learning experience that both challenges students and develops teamwork. While learning important concepts about our legal system and honing communication skills, they will be practicing higher-level thinking skills. Throughout the course of the unit your students will be involved and enthusiastic. What more could a teacher ask for?

Part 1

Building a Foundation

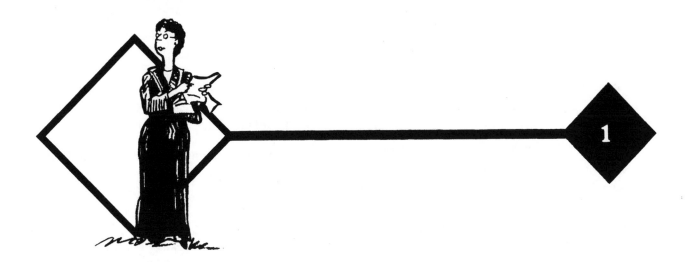

Understanding the Judicial System

The Judicial System and Schools

Ever since the ancient Greeks, civilizations have sought to bring to justice those individuals or groups believed to have broken society's rules. They may have been charged with committing a crime against laws written by governing bodies, or they may have been perceived as violating the civil rights of others.

Through personal experiences and the media, today's students are exposed to the judicial process to a greater extent than ever before. Hence, one of the challenges teachers face is to help pupils understand the complexities of the U.S. legal system.

When teaching a U.S. government curriculum, teachers can usually provide students with many practical examples of how the executive and legislative branches of government operate. Classroom elections and student government meetings offer the opportunity for students to experience how these branches work. Indeed, the administration and faculty are themselves examples of the executive branch, and decision making by students in the classroom is, to a certain extent, legislative activity.

Sorely lacking in most curricula is an in-depth study of the U.S. judicial system. Unfortunately, the perception of the mechanics of how the jury system works is often formed by fictional trials depicted in movies or on TV, where justice triumphs through some miraculous last-minute revelation. The planning, hard work, and knowledge necessary to bring a case to trial are glossed over.

A Challenging Curriculum

As teachers, we can read about the trial process, or we can provide students with opportunities to experience the challenges each side faces in bring a trial to court. Mock trials are the perfect vehicles for allowing this to happen. When working with the evidence and statements of witnesses, students use higher-level thinking skills to plan their strategies and represent the best possible case for their side. The importance of inferential reading skills becomes readily evident. Cooperative learning takes place naturally. Teamwork, which is usually associated with the athletic field, becomes an absolute necessity if a side is to present its case most effectively. As students plan their mock trials, they learn how to evaluate evidence and formulate questions so they can present their case in the best possible light.

Although a jury verdict in its favor might seem to indicate a win for a team, students soon realize that in some instances, no matter how well they have planned their legal strategies, their side is not likely to win.

Students as Attorneys

Aspiring lawyers spend three years in law school. During that time, they participate in a number of mock trials (such as moot court, competitions, practice court, and trial advocacy classes). Even after obtaining a law degree and becoming a trial attorney, it may be some time before the new lawyer actually serves as the lead counsel for a case. The fact that an individual's freedom or civil right is at stake demands that attorneys have experience in hypothetical cases and in assisting other attorneys before they assume the actual responsibility of trying a case themselves.

Obviously, we cannot expect students to perform as professional attorneys with the amount of training they can receive in a classroom setting. We can, however, make them aware of what is involved in the judicial procedure to help them understand the many hours of preparation that go into a trial before it actually reaches the courtroom. By learning how our court system works, students will have a better understanding of judicial decisions that affect their lives.

Famous Real Cases

In the famous *Scopes* trial, John T. Scopes, a high school teacher, was charged with violating Tennessee law by teaching evolution.

Famous murder trials include the Lindbergh kidnaping trial in which Bruno Hauptmann was charged with the murder of aviator Charles Lindbergh's baby son. Hauptmann was convicted and later executed. Another notable murder trial was the Leopold-Loeb case, in which the defendants confessed to killing their cousins, Bobby Franks. They were saved from the gallows by the eloquence of lawyer Clarence Darrow. More recently, former football player O.J. Simpson has been the object of worldwide attention, both in winning an acquittal in the criminal murder trial in which he was accused of killing his former wife and her friend and in losing in the subsequent civil trial brought by members of the victims' families.

Decisions handed down by the U.S. Supreme Court have played a major role in changing our society. The *Dred Scott* decision in 1857 was a major setback for slaves seeking their freedom. Scott, who lived in the Minnesota Territory, sued for his freedom based on the Missouri Compromise of 1820, which prohibited slavery in federal territories. The Supreme Court declared the already-repealed Compromise unconstitutional because it deprived a person of his personal property – a slave – without due process of law. It further stated that African Americans who were descendants of slaves had no rights as American citizens. Fortunately, this Court decision was invalidated by the passage of the Fourteenth Amendment in 1868.

In *Plessy v. Ferguson* in 1896 the Court declared that restrictions on a person's use of public schools and public accommodations, such as hotels, restaurants, and transportation facilities based on ethnicity, was legal. It was not until the 1950s that the Civil Rights movement forced a change. The decision in *Brown v. Board of Education of Topeka* in 1954 struck a major blow for school desegregation.

Undoubtedly, students have seen an individual being read his or her rights to remain silent and to have an attorney present for questioning. This milestone in civil rights is the result of the U.S. Supreme Court decision in *Miranda v. Arizona.* (1966).

Clearly, court cases such as these paint a portrait of the historical context in which they were tried. Their relevance is in the influence they have on our everyday lives. As a middle school teacher, you can bring the judicial system to life by showing students the impact judicial rulings continue to have on society today. The mock trial is the perfect means by which to do this.

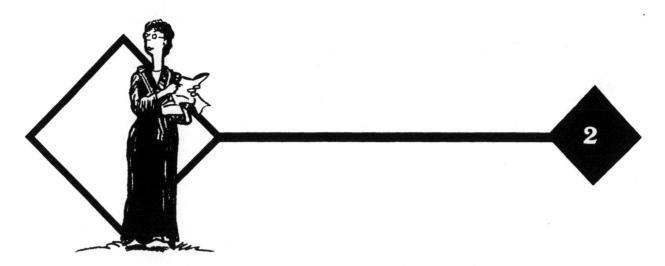

Court Systems of the United States

One of the chief purposes of government, according to the U.S. Constitution, is to ensure domestic tranquillity. The primary function of every court system is to fulfill the promises of peace and order implied in the Constitution. The courts, as part of the judicial branch of government, seek to resolve problems arising out of civil and criminal law. Were it not for these courts, an atmosphere of violence and anarchy might prevail.

The U.S. court system is one of the most complex in the world, with courts on almost every level of government. Each state has a supreme court, courts of appeal, and courts of lower jurisdiction, that handle minor civil and criminal offenses. The highest court in the land is, of course, the U.S. Supreme Court. The following diagram gives a general idea of how the U.S. court system is structured.

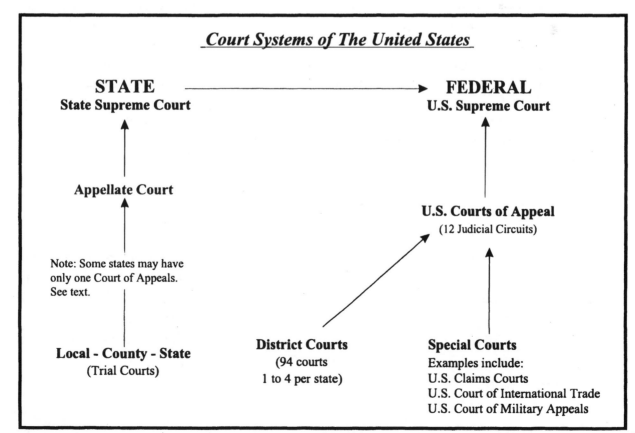

Court Systems of The United States

STATE ⟶ **FEDERAL**

State Supreme Court — U.S. Supreme Court

Appellate Court

U.S. Courts of Appeal
(12 Judicial Circuits)

Note: Some states may have only one Court of Appeals. See text.

Local - County - State
(Trial Courts)

District Courts
(94 courts
1 to 4 per state)

Special Courts
Examples include:
U.S. Claims Courts
U.S. Court of International Trade
U.S. Court of Military Appeals

DOI: 10.4324/9781003236092-2

State Courts

As stated above, each of the fifty states has its own court system, which typically consists of trial courts and appellate courts, including a state supreme court.

Trial Courts

Also known as "trials of first instance," trial courts deal with parties in conflict, hear **witnesses**, review **evidence** and facts, and reach a decision or verdict. These courts may be divided further into criminal courts and civil courts.

- **Criminal courts** handle cases in which individuals are accused of a crime. The trial may be heard before a jury, or the defendant may elect to have the judge decide the verdict. If the defendant is judged guilty, the punishment will vary, depending on the severity of the crime and other factors such as a prior criminal record

- **Civil courts** deal with private disputes between individuals or corporations. The public is not involved in civil actions, and the state does not prosecute them as it does criminal cases. The object of a civil case in which the defendant is judged to be wrong is to attempt to restore the situation to what it might have been had no legal wrong been committed. In many instances, the defendant may have to pay money to the wronged party. These are called **compensatory damages**. **Punitive damages** are sometimes awarded against a defendant to punish him or her and to let the community know that such behavior will not be tolerated.

Court systems governing trial courts may vary widely from place to place. Major population centers may have courts of general jurisdiction, but to expedite matters, they may be organized into special branches such as criminal, civil, traffic, and juvenile courts. In many areas, these courts are known as **inferior courts**. They handle minor civil and criminal cases (such as **misdemeanors** and minor **felonies**). They may also handle preliminary parts of more serious criminal cases such as setting bail, advising the accused of his or her rights, appointing defense counsel, and deciding whether evidence justifies holding a defendant for a trial in a higher or **superior court**.

Appellate Courts and Supreme Courts

Appellate courts handle cases in which the fairness of the lower court's decision is in question. Most states refer to their highest court as a supreme court. New York is a notable exception, calling its highest court the Court of Appeals and using the designation of "supreme court" for lower courts. Some states do not have intermediate appellate courts.

Joshua Bartholomew has been arrested in Midville. His is accused of armed robbery of a Midville convenience store. After reviewing the evidence, the municipal judge has set bail, and Mr. Bartholomew is sent to the local jail until bail can be posted. Mr. Bartholomew has retained the services of a local attorney (had he been unable to do so because of insufficient financial resources, a court-appointed attorney would have been named). Because of the seriousness of the charges against the defendant, the trial is transferred to a higher or superior court.

In our case, Joshua Bartholomew, the defendant who was charged with armed robbery, has been found guilty by the jury hearing the trial. The judge has sentenced Mr. Bartholomew to the state penitentiary. Mr. Bartholomew's attorney is appealing the verdict on the grounds that the judge made errors during the trial; that is, the judge did not allow several pieces of evidence to be introduced that would have been favorable to the defendant. The appellate court will review the case and, if it believes that this evidence should have been admitted, will probably order that the case be retried. The original judge may preside at the retrial unless some particular bias was shown or unless the judge is no longer assigned to the court.

Appellate courts are usually presided over by several judges, whereas trial courts have only one judge. The higher the court, the greater the force of its decision. The decision of an appellate court is binding within its jurisdiction, meaning that the rules it lays down must be followed by lower courts when faced with the same issue.

A party involved in a trial in a lower court who believes that the trial ruling was wrong may file an appeal. An exception would be in a case of an acquittal of a defendant accused of murder. If this individual was found not guilty, the state cannot appeal the verdict or retry the defendant.

Federal Courts

Federal courts were created in accordance with Article III of the Constitution. These include the special district, circuit, and supreme courts of our federal government.

Special Courts

Special courts include the following:

- **The U.S. Claims Court** - This court has jurisdiction over monetary claims against the United States based on the Constitution or acts of Congress.

- **The U.S. Court of International Trade** - This court has jurisdiction over civil actions against the United States involving federal laws governing imports.

- **The U.S. Court of Military Appeals** - This court reviews court martial convictions for all the armed services. It is subject to review by the U.S. Supreme Court only in a limited number of cases.

District Courts

District Courts are the trial courts of general federal jurisdiction. They hear all matters that relate to federal laws and, in some cases, that involve U.S. Citizens of different states. There are 94 district courts, with between one and four in each state and one in the District of Columbia. States with larger populations such as California, Texas, and New York have four courts each. Usually one judge presides, but in some cases three judges are required to make up the court.

U.S. Courts of Appeal

These courts were created to relieve the U.S. Supreme Court of having to review all trials originally decided by federal courts. Decisions of these courts are final except when law provides for direct review by the Supreme Court. Twelve judicial circuits compose the courts of appeal system, and each of the 50 states and the District of Columbia is assigned to one of them.

A case that reached the U.S. Supreme Court was Griffin v. California (1965). Griffin was convicted of murder in the first degree in a jury trial in a California court. He did not testify at the trial. The Fifth Amendment of the U.S. Constitution states that no person "shall be compelled in any criminal case to be a witness against himself." The prosecutor made much of the failure of the defendant to testify, inferring that this proved his guilt. The trial court judge instructed the jury that it was the defendant's constitutional right not to testify; however, he went on to state that the jury could take this failure to testify into consideration. The defendant was found guilty and sentenced to death. The California Supreme Court upheld the conviction. Because the appeal was based on a constitutional issue, the case was sent to the U.S. Supreme Court. The Supreme Court reversed the lower court's ruling. As a result of the Supreme Court ruling, the case was remanded for a new trial with the proper instructions read to the jury.

U.S. Supreme Court

The highest court in the land is composed of nine Supreme Court justices, one of who is named the Chief Justice. In both civil and criminal law, the Supreme Court is the ultimate court of appeal. All other remedies must be exhausted before the Court can be petitioned for appeal or review of a lower court decision. Cases originating in state courts can be appealed to the Court directly from state supreme courts; cases originating in federal court must first go through the U.S. District Court and the U.S. Courts of Appeal. The court itself decides whether to hear a case or let the decision of the lower court stand. In all cases, the Court will decline to review decision lacking the substantial federal issue.

Although this description of the U.S. Court system is simplified, it serves effectively as a basic introduction to its structure. Remember that the structure of the court system may vary from state to state, and the names of the courts on similar levels may also be different. Check to see how your state judicial system may vary from what is presented here. Make those adjustments in our presentation to your class.

Part 2

Structuring the Mock Trial

Planning Your Mock Trial

Planning your first mock trial can be a bit daunting, but with a little bit of effort, organization, and preparation, it can be an enjoyable and rich educational experience.

Suggestions are offered here for choosing participants for your trial and preparing your audience. A sample schedule for planning your trial is also included, as are possible community resources. These suggestions are by no means all-inclusive, but they should give you an outline of what to do before and during your mock trial.

Principal Participants

- **Attorneys** (2-6)

  You will need a minimum of one attorney for each side; two to three attorneys per side works best. The tasks of delivering opening and closing statements and conducting direct and cross-examinations can be overwhelming for one student. In addition, should a student be absent, other attorneys can assume his or her duties.

- **Witnesses** (6-8)

  Three or four witnesses for each side works best. Less than three will not allow the class to fully develop the case. More than four will drag out the activity too long. Students should be chosen for these parts based on their ability and willingness to take on the identity of the witness they portray. Ask, "How would this individual think and speak? What background would such a person have?" By "becoming" the witness, the student will be much better able to handle cross-examination questions. The students should try to anticipate what each witness might be asked on cross-examination. All witnesses should participate in the formulation of direct examination questions and can assist attorneys in formulating cross-examination questions for the opposition.

DOI: 10.4324/9781003236092-3

Other Participants

Not every student is going to want to be in the limelight for the mock trial. Many individuals play important roles in bringing a case to trial. The following are important roles that may be used in each trial.

- **Bailiff**

   This individual sees to it that the courtroom is set up properly and guides jurors and those watching the trial to their seats.

- **Court Reporter**

   Because your students will not have the skills of a court reporter at their disposal, an audiotape can serve as the official transcript of the trial. One student (the court reporter) should be in charge of operating the tape recorder.

- **Television Camera Operators (2-3)**

   Now that television cameras are allowed in many courtrooms, a video recording can be made of the proceedings. The camera should be in a fixed position in a place that will permit the audience to view the judge, the attorneys, and the witnesses. The student camera operators should take care that microphones pick up the voices of the trial participants only.

- **Research Assistants (2-4)**

   In some cases, students may need to research facts given in affidavits. For example, if a witness qualifies as an expert, student research assistants could try to find out more information about the witness's area of expertise.

   These student research assistants could also create charts, diagrams, and floor plans or site plans of crime scenes. By letting the students decide which items to use as evidence, the mock trial experience is closer to a real-life situation. To be effective, any visual aids must be large enough for the jury to see in the courtroom setting. Remind your assistants that it is not advisable or permissible to bring weapons or facsimiles to school. Review your school's regulations carefully and pass this information on to students.

- **Jurors (6 jurors and 2 alternates)**

   When choosing jurors, it is important to select from people who have had as little access to trial information as possible. It is usually best to use students from another class as your jury pool. The identities of the jurors should not be divulged until immediately before the trial. When the jury is impaneled, the two alternatives sit with the six jurors to hear the trial. When the jurors leave to deliberate, the two alternates are excused. It should be explained that the alternates are necessary in case one of the six jurors cannot remain for the whole trial. The alternates should be designated "Number 1" and "Number 2" when they are selected and serve in that order if necessary. Prior to the trial, be sure to have an area reserved where the jury can deliberate in private.

- **Audience**

   The best audience is a class that is not familiar with the trial. An audience is not essential; however, it serves to enlarge the group of students who learn about the judicial system and adds to the authenticity of the courtroom setting. When using an audience, it is wise to do a briefing with the visiting class the day before the trial. Describe the basic facts of the trial and courtroom procedures. Use the guidelines on page 19 to review what information should be shared with the audience.

Audience Briefing

Statement of Facts

Tell students the basic facts of the trial. Be sure to give no more information than is contained in the trial's Statement of Facts. Do not give the names of students who will be the attorneys or will take on the personas of the witnesses.

Jury Selection

Inform students that members of the class will be chosen to serve on the jury; however, they will not know who has been chosen until immediately before the trial. There will be six jurors and two alternates. The alternates will sit in the jury box. If any of the original six jurors cannot be available for deliberation, one of the alternates will be called on as the replacement. When the jury deliberations begin, the alternates are excused. The first of the six jurors called will act as the jury foreperson and will serve as spokesperson for the group.

Courtroom Procedure

Students should be aware that this trial will follow the format of an actual trial and that the following courtroom rules will apply:

1. All participants and observers rise when the judge enters the courtroom.

2. The judge instructs the jury about the trial it is about to hear.

3. **Opening statements** will be given by attorneys for the **prosecution/plaintiff** and for the defense.

4. Attorney(s) for the prosecution/plaintiff will begin direct questioning of the witnesses. After each witness is questioned, attorney(s) for the defense may cross examine.

5. Attorney(s) for the defense will begin direct questioning of the witnesses for the defense. After each witness is questioned, attorneys for the plaintiff/prosecution may cross-examine.

6. After each side has completed its questioning, attorneys for each side will give summations or closing statements.

7. The jury will deliberate. After it has reached a verdict, it will be led back into the courtroom by the bailiff. The judge will ask if the jury has reached a verdict, and the foreperson will answer, "We have, your honor." The judge may ask to see the verdict in writing or may ask the foreperson to state the jury's decision.

In a criminal case, the jury must reach a unanimous decision on the guilt or innocence of the defendant. If any juror has a reasonable doubt of guilt, the defendant must be judged not guilty.

In a civil trial, a unanimous decision is not required. In most states, four or five of the six jurors must agree for a verdict to be reached. Check your local courts to find out what procedure they follow. The decision is based on a **preponderance of the evidence**.

Note: The opposing sides in the mock trial will not have met prior to the court appearance. They have prepared questions for their own witnesses but do not know what may be asked of their witnesses on cross-examination. **This is not a play**. Neither side knows what the opposition has prepared in terms of direct or cross-examination questions.

Hints for a More Effective Trial

Work Independently

When preparing for your mock trial, ensure that the two sides work independently. Although the witnesses will know the questions that will be asked on direct examination, as in real trials, they will not know what will be asked on cross-examination. It is, therefore, important that each attorney and witness try to anticipate what questions might be asked on cross-examination. Each side should also be aware that any information discussed in strategy sessions should be treated confidentially. To ensure that trial materials are not circulated, do not allow students to take them out of the classroom. If the opposition is aware of information or strategies, the element of surprise is lost.

As an example, we had a mock trial in which the defendant was identified by a prosecution witness who had seen him through a curtained window. The defendant's attorney stated that if the window had a curtain, identification could not be made. The prosecution witness said he had a clear view of the robber's face because the curtain was café style and only came halfway up the window. The defense was clearly at a disadvantage, having made no attempt to identify the curtain style.

Advise students working with the witness affidavits to look for minor, often overlooked details that can work to their advantage. Each case has been designed to have weaknesses for both sides.

Attorney Preparation

Instruct the student attorneys that their opening statements can be written beforehand and read to the jury. Attorneys can also have direct examination questions in hand while questioning their witnesses. Although cross-examination questions and closing statements can also be prepared before the trial, the attorneys should be aware of information given in court that might lead to additional cross-examination questions and that might prompt changes and additions to the closing statements.

Plan, Plan, Plan

In an activity of this nature, planning is everything. Follow the schedule outlined on page 22. Be organized but flexible. Allow extra time to schedule outside professionals to talk to your class and to accommodate unforeseen events.

Community Involvement

You will not find it difficult to involve law enforcement professionals in your mock trial. One word of caution: These individuals are very busy. Allow plenty of time for them to arrange their schedules to accommodate you. If you would like to have professionals work with your students, contact them at least four to six weeks before you hope to start your trial. You might consider contacting the following sources:

- **Local Police Chief or Sheriff**
  Police personnel can be invaluable. If they can't answer a question or help you with a problem, they can often direct you to someone who can.

- **Local Attorneys**
  Many attorneys will be more than happy to talk to your students about the legal system and help with formulating direct and cross-examination questions. You may be able to convince an attorney to act as the judge in your trials.

■ **Bar Associations**

Contact you county bar association to see if your state bar association is one of the many that hold mock trial competitions on the high school level. If so, the association may be able to send you materials on these trials and perhaps a video of the trial competition. This would allow your students to see a mock trial in progress. Be aware that some of the subject matter covered in these trials may not be suitable for younger students. Some bar associations have programs for elementary and middle school students, although they probably will not involve actual mock trials at this level.

■ **County Courthouse**

Check with the nearest courthouse to see if you can arrange a field trip. Such trips are usually quite popular and have to be arranged several months in advance. Touring a courthouse allows students to see courtroom procedures in action. Unfortunately, you will not know what students will see until the day of your trip. Cases that will be available for viewing on any given day will depend on what trials or activities are scheduled.

Sample Planning Schedule

Number of sessions (45 minutes each)	Concepts or Activities
1	Review structure of the legal system Differentiate between civil and criminal trials Identify participants in the trial and the roles they play
1 to 2	Explain courtroom procedures Introduce simplified rules of evidence Distinguish between questions used in direct examination and cross-examination
1 to 2	Read the Statement of Facts and affidavits for the specific case to be used as the basis for your trial
2	Assign roles to individual students Have students prepare direct examination questions Have students prepare exhibits (charts, reports, letters) that might be necessary for the trial
2	Have students prepare cross-examination questions for the opposition Have students try to anticipate which questions the opposition may ask in cross-examination Have students continue preparation of exhibits
1	Have students write opening and closing statements
2	Have students practice direct examination questions for each side Have students review possible cross-examination questions their witnesses might be asked Have students review cross-examination questions for the opposition and anticipate what their answers might be Have students practice delivery of opening and closing statements Have students, if possible, visit the courtroom to familiarize themselves with the setting
2 to 3	Choose and impanel a jury Stage the mock trial After the trial, discuss the results with the jury and spectators
1 to 2	With the mock trial participants: • view the video tape of the trial • evaluate trial specifics

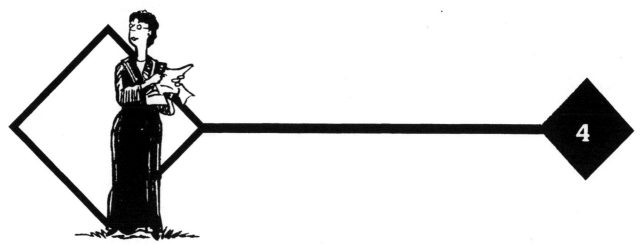

Conducting a Mock Trial

Certain procedures and rules are standard when conducting any trial. The following materials are presented in a format that is easy for students to understand. The suggested courtroom layout is similar to that used in courtrooms throughout the country. It is simple to set up in your classroom or in a roomier environment such as an auditorium if you expect of have a larger audience. Don't overlook the possibility that your local municipal court may be available to you.

The "Anatomy of a Trial" section will take you step by step through the various stages of your trial. This includes courtroom procedure and the order in which opening statements, questioning of witnesses, and closing arguments are made.

"Rules of Evidence and Procedure" gives detailed information for formulating questions and presenting evidence. In addition, examples of opening and closing statements are included.

If possible, duplicate all or part of the materials on pages 24 - 33 for your students. This information can serve as your text for teaching about these areas and makes an excellent reference source should questions arise as your mock trial planning gets under way.

When presenting trial materials found in Chapters 5 and 6, you may read or paraphrase the background information and historical information, but you should **not** duplicate this material and hand it out to students to read for themselves. Students should get all the facts for the cases from the statements of fact and affidavits. Additional information (especially in the Booth and the Romeo and Juliet cases) can result in confusion. You may, however, share the definitions, exhibits and lists of participants if you feel this would be helpful.

Figure 4.1.
Typical Courtroom Layout.

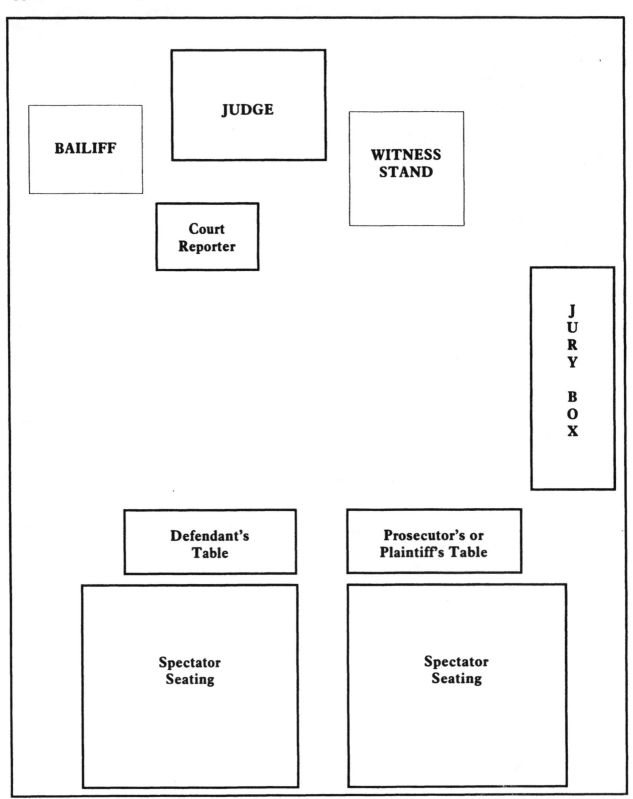

Anatomy of a Trial

Court Session Begins

The bailiff calls the Court to order.

Example: "All rise, the Court for the City of Riverton is now in session, the Honorable [judge's name] presiding."

The judge enters, and all participants remain standing until the judge instructs them to be seated.

The judge announces the case.

Example: "The court will now hear the case of _____ v. _____."

The judge tells the jury the specific facts of the case and then asks the attorneys if they are ready to present their cases.

Opening Statements

The attorneys for each side make their opening statements to the jury.

Prosecution (Criminal Case) or Plaintiff (Civil Case)

The prosecutor or the plaintiff's attorney summarizes the evidence that will be presented to prove the charge made against the defendant.

Defense

The defendant's attorney summarizes the evidence that will be presented in answer to the charge.

Direct Examination by the Prosecutor or the Plaintiff's Attorney

The prosecutor or plaintiff's attorney will call to the stand the witnesses to support its case. Direct examination allows witnesses to answer questions in narrative form and present facts and evidence to support and prove the case.

Cross-Examination by the Defendant's Attorney

The defendant's attorney may cross-examine each witness after the prosecutor or plaintiff's attorney has completed direct examination. The purpose of cross-examination is to clarify or cast doubt on the testimony of opposing witnesses. Only information presented in sworn affidavits and in direct examination testimony can be used as the basis of cross-examination questions.

Direct Examination by the Defendant's Attorney

The defendant's attorney will call to the stand the witnesses to support its case. The defendant may or may not take the stand. The direct examination format is similar to that used for the prosecution's or plaintiff's witnesses.

Cross-Examination by the Prosecutor or the Plaintiff's Attorney

Cross-examination of defense witnesses follows the pattern used in cross-examination of the prosecution's or the plaintiff's witnesses.

Closing Arguments

After both sides have presented their evidence, each side's attorney presents a closing argument to the jury.

Prosecution or Plaintiff

The attorney reviews the evidence presented and points out how the evidence and testimony presented support the charge against the defendant. Any law applicable in the case is also presented. The prosecutor asks for a finding of "guilty"; in a civil trial, the plaintiff's attorney asks the jury to find in favor of the plaintiff.

Defense

The attorney for the defense also reviews the evidence presented, pointing out how it *does not* support the charge or claim against the defendant. The attorney for the defendant asks for a verdict of "not guilty" in a criminal case or to find in favor of the defense in a civil case.

Rendering a Verdict

The mock trial jury consists of six members plus two alternates. If the alternates are not needed, the judge dismisses them before deliberations begin.

Criminal Trial

In a criminal trial, the burden of proof rests with the prosecution. It must prove "beyond a reasonable doubt" that the defendant is guilty of the crime. The verdict of the jury must be unanimous.

Civil Trial

The jury in a civil trial must weigh the evidence. A decision should be based on the preponderance of the evidence. The jury must decide whether the evidence supports the plaintiff's or the defendant's claim. A verdict need not be unanimous but must be agreed to by five of the six jurors. Sometimes the jury is asked to place a monetary value on a decision that is rendered in favor of a plaintiff. In some cases, the judge may issue an injunction ordering an individual to refrain from doing a specific act.

Rules of Evidence and Procedure

Lawyers spend many years training for the day when they will try a case in the courtroom. Procedures can be quite complicated. The following materials list rules for questioning and presenting evidence that have been modified for our mock trial participants.

Direct Examination

Form of Questions. Witnesses cannot be asked leading questions by the attorney who calls them to the stand. A leading question is one in which the attorney supplies information with the intent of eliciting a "yes" or "no" answer. Direct questions are usually phrased to elicit facts from the witness. They usually begin with such words as *how, where, when, why, explain*.

> *Example of a direct question:* "Mrs. Smith, where did you live before you moved to New Haven?"

> *Example of a leading question:* "Mrs. Smith, isn't it true that you lived at 403 Main Street in Appleton before you moved to New Haven?"

The purpose of direct examination is to have the witness narrate a story; however, care must be taken to ask for specific information.

> *Example of a narrative question:* "Mrs. Smith, why did you move to New Haven?"

Scope of Witness Examination. Direct examination can cover all of the facts relevant to the case of which the witness has firsthand knowledge. For mock trial purposes, information contained in the witness affidavits may be used as a basis for determining those relevant facts of which the witness has firsthand knowledge.

Cross-Examination

Form of Questions. An attorney can ask leading questions when cross-examining the opponent's witnesses. Narrative questions should be avoided. Attorneys should be careful not to ask a question on cross-examination if they do not know what the witness's answer will be.

> *Example of a leading question:* "Mr. Tompkins, you had a lot to gain if Mr. Sherman lost his job, didn't you?"

Scope of Witness Examination. Attorneys can ask questions only about information brought out in direct examination or relating to the credibility of the witness. For mock trial purposes, questions can be asked on cross-examination about any information that is in a witness's affidavit.

Impeachment. The attorney conducting the cross-examination may want to show that the witness should not be believed. This can be done by asking questions that make the witness's truth-telling ability suspect.

Refreshing Recollection. Impeachment can also be done by introducing the witness's affidavit and having the witness read the portion of the affidavit that was contradicted on direct examination. The witness can then be questioned about any discrepancies.

Additional Rules of Evidence and Procedure

Hearsay

Hearsay is any statement made by someone not present in the court that is offered as proof of a fact. Hearsay is not permitted.

Example: A witness states, "The people in my office have told me that Mrs. Lee was fired from her past job because she was always absent."

Opinions of Witnesses

Usually, witnesses are not allowed to state their opinions. An exception to this rule is a witness who is qualified as an "expert." The attorney who calls this witness is the one who must bring out on direct examination the background that would qualify the witness as an expert.

Relevance of Evidence

Only testimony and physical evidence that is important to the case can be presented.

Example: An attorney may ask a witness's age on cross-examination only if it is relevant to the case.

Introduction of Physical Evidence

Only objects, documents, and other physical pieces of evidence that are relevant to the case can be introduced. Before the trial, each side must permit the opposing side to examine any piece of evidence or any **exhibit** that will be introduced. During the actual trial, each piece of evidence is introduced immediately prior to its use in questioning. The attorney presents the evidence to the judge: "Your Honor, I offer this letter for admission as evidence." At this point, the judge will examine the evidence and label it (P [number] for the prosecution or plaintiff, or D [number] for the defense). The exhibit is then returned to the attorney, who will show it to the opposing attorney. At this point, questioning of the witness can continue. Affidavits are not admissible as evidence but may be used during cross-examination for impeachment purposes.

Objections

Attorneys can object at any time they believe the opposition has violated the rules of evidence. *Objections are made directly to the judge and must be made immediately at the time the attorney believes the violation has occurred.* Some of the standard objections that can be made include the following:

Irrelevant evidence: "I object, Your Honor. This testimony is irrelevant to the facts of the case."

Leading question: "Objection. Counsel is leading the witness." (This objection may only be used if an attorney is using leading questions on direct examination.)

Hearsay: "Objection. The question (or answer) is based on hearsay."

Opinion: "Objection. Counsel is asking the witness to give an opinion."

Because mock trials move very rapidly, it is difficult for student lawyers to gain experience in being able to recognize testimony that might be subject to an objection. To help them become more proficient in this area, you might consider having the students practice with testimony that would elicit objections.

Opening Statements

The purpose of the opening statement is to introduce to the jury the facts of the trial. The prosecutor or the plaintiff's attorney will present the reasons why the defendant was charged. When stating the facts, he or she will use wording intended to reflect positively on his or her viewpoint of the action taken. Conversely, the defendant's lawyer will present the case in support of his or her client(s). Both attorneys will tell the jury which witnesses they will introduce and what they hope will be the verdict.

Closing Statements

When the attorneys present their closing statements, they review the facts that have been presented and reinforce why the facts they have presented support their side. They also, whenever possible, refute the opposition's viewpoint. Finally, they ask that the jury find in their favor. For mock trial purposes, each opening and closing statement should be between two and five minutes in length.

Examples of Opening and Closing Statements

The following are examples of opening and closing statements that might have been presented in the case of *Horace Singleton v. ABC Construction Company*. For demonstration purposes, we have given the opening statement as it might be presented by the plaintiff's attorney and the closing statement as it might be presented by the defendant's lawyer. Remember that each side delivers an opening and closing statement.

IN THE CIRCUIT COURT OF
THE THIRD JUDICIAL CIRCUIT
IN AND FOR LEE COUNTY, _____

HORACE SINGLETON,
  Plaintiff,

-v-

ABC CONSTRUCTION COMPANY,
  Defendant

CASE NO.: 97-321CA

STATEMENT OF FACTS

    Horace Singleton hired ABC Construction Co. to build a deck onto the back of his house at 123 Elm Street, Milltown. John Carpenter, the owner of ABC Construction Co., presented plans to Mr. Singleton. After discussing construction methods, the parties signed a contract in the amount of $4,500 for completion of the work. The contract specified materials and guaranteed the work as far as workmanship and structural integrity were concerned for a period of three years. Because of the slope of the land in the back of Mr. Singleton's house, it was necessary for the deck to be constructed with support posts to the rear of the deck. These beams were 4 feet, 5 inches in height. Surrounding the deck was a railing 3 feet, 6 inches above the floor of the deck. There were large posts at each corner of the railing and intermediate support posts with 4-inch spaces between them.

    Two months after the work was completed, Mr. Singleton had a party at his house. Mr. Singleton claims that, during the party, one of his guests, Mr. Jimbo Robins, leaned on the railing. It broke under his weight. Mr. Singleton is suing ABC Construction Co. for damages, specifying that the railing gave way because of faulty construction and poor quality materials. ABC states that it collapsed because Mr. Singleton had made alterations to the work and in so doing weakened the railing, allowing it to break when Mr. Robins leaned on it. ABC also claims that, because Mr. Singleton made alterations to the railing, the warranty that ABC had given for three years was no longer in effect.

Sample Opening Statement of Plaintiff's Attorney

Ladies and gentlemen, last March, Mr. Horace Singleton signed a contract with ABC Construction Company to build a deck on the rear of his house. He had seen their truck in the neighborhood, so he decided to call them to build this addition. Mr. Singleton made a big mistake. He did not check to see if ABC Construction Company had satisfied customers. As it turns out, finding a satisfied customer of ABC Construction Company is easier said than done.

When he called John Carpenter, the owner of ABC, to discuss the work, Mr. Carpenter told him that his company had built more than 200 decks in the last two years. He assured Mr. Singleton that his company had the necessary experience. After looking over several stock plans, a contract was signed. The work was begun on April 5th and completed on April 10th. Mrs. Singleton, who was at home during the construction period, stated that at no time did she see Mr. Carpenter visit the job. Upon completion of the work, ABC Construction Company was paid in full.

About a week later, Mr. Singleton noted that one of the intermediate posts supporting the railing was loose. He called ABC and was assured that the post would be fixed. When 10 days had gone by and no one from ABC had come to make the repair, Mr. Singleton called again. After another week, Mr. Singleton decided to make the repair himself. He and his wife were hosting a gathering the following weekend, and they wanted to make sure that the deck looked good for their visitors. When making the repair, he discovered that not only were some of the posts not nailed properly, but some of them were not plumb or straight. He also corrected these deficiencies. Mr. Singleton readily admits that he made alterations; however, we will prove that the railing in question broke because it was poorly constructed and made of defective and inferior materials.

When Mr. and Mrs. Singleton's guests arrived on the day of the gathering, the Singletons received favorable comments about the new deck; however, when the guests were told about the company that had done the work, several said they had heard the company did not have a good reputation. As the evening wore on, one of the guests, Jimbo Robins, a catcher for the Charlestown Shooflies, leaned on the deck railing. It gave way, and Mr. Robins fell off the back of the deck, breaking his throwing arm.

You will hear testimony today that ABC Construction Company is guilty of shoddy workmanship—that by completing the work in such a short time, they rushed the job at the expense of using safe building techniques. Mr. James Woods, owner of Woods Builders and president of the local builders association, will tell you that ABC Construction Company, which is not a member of the association, has not practiced safe construction techniques and has been known to buy inferior materials. He will show how the only way the railing could have broken under Mr. Robins's weight was if inferior quality materials and workmanship were a part of the initial construction. Mr. Woods will state that Mr. Carpenter was known to rarely visit a job site once he signed a contract. He will state, moreover, that the workers constructing the deck were inexperienced and that ABC Construction had a high employee turnover. In addition, you will hear from Dory Cavanaugh, who will relate the experience she had with ABC when she had her garage built.

We are sure that after you hear our witnesses' experiences with ABC Construction Company, you will agree that they should be held liable for the damage to Mr. Singleton's deck and should be held accountable to make repairs that will pass the inspection of an expert in the field of construction.

In addition, we're sure you will agree that Mr. Jimbo Robins should receive compensation for his injuries and the loss of pay during the six weeks it took his arm to heal. After hearing the testimony from all of the witnesses today, we're sure you will agree that you, the members of the jury, should find for the plaintiff.

Sample Closing Statement of Defendant's Attorney

Ladies and gentlemen, the plaintiff would have you believe that ABC Construction Company is guilty of allowing shoddy workmanship and of buying inferior materials, and that it has a poor reputation in the community. We have proved that nothing could be further from the truth. We have presented as evidence letters from homeowners who are delighted with their experiences in dealing with ABC Construction Company. You have seen invoices from the Ajax Lumber Company, which show that materials delivered to the Singleton job were top grade. Ajax has an excellent reputation and provides building materials for most construction companies in the area, including that of Mr. James Woods, the local builders association president.

You have seen that John Carpenter, ABC's founder, has built his company from a small operation to one that has grown considerably. In many companies this size, the owner would hire someone to contact prospective customers and help them plan the additions and improvements to their homes, but Mr. Carpenter realizes that when someone wishes to make a major change in his or her home, this is a big investment. He continues, as he did when he first started ABC Construction, to give his personal touch to each project. As you have seen, this company is very large, and Mr. Carpenter cannot be everywhere to supervise all of the many jobs the company has. As with all good leaders, he has delegated authority to knowledgeable people in the field of construction.

You have heard the testimony of Mr. James Woods of the local builders association. Upon questioning, Mr. Woods acknowledged that his company, Woods Builders, is a competitor of ABC Construction Company. He further stated that the builders association is made up of a select few companies in the area who have chosen to band together for mutual profit. We have also shown that Mr. Woods's comments concerning ABC are not admissible as evidence as they are hearsay. In fact, Mr. Woods has not inspected any of ABC's projects and is not able to give an expert opinion.

ABC Construction Company has no record of Mr. Singleton's so-called first call. After receiving what Mr. Singleton claims was his second call, arrangements were made to investigate the problem. When ABC's construction superintendent arrived on the job, he noted that several of the support posts and the main corner posts had been damaged and had hammer marks on them where they had been hit in an apparent attempt to straighten them. Mr. Singleton readily admits that he was impatient and that he fixed the problem himself. He obviously is not an experienced carpenter. Had he been, he would probably have built the deck himself. When he attempted to make the repairs, he damaged the structural integrity of the deck. The guarantee for workmanship on the deck was voided when Mr. Singleton attempted to "fix the problem." He now says that ABC Construction should be responsible for a problem he himself created.

We're sure you will agree that it is unfair to expect ABC to pay for repairing a deck that was damaged by a customer's crude attempt at carpentry. In addition, we know you will agree that Mr. Robins's injuries cannot be blamed on ABC's workmanship but rather on Mr. Singleton's so-called repairs.

Preparing Students to Begin a Mock Trial

After reviewing the "Sample Opening Statement of the Plaintiff's Attorney" and the "Sample Closing Statement of the Defendant's Attorney," the differing viewpoints should be readily apparent. The plaintiff's attorney asserts that at no time did Mrs. Singleton see Mr. Carpenter visit the job site. The defendant's attorney counters that Mr. Carpenter cannot be everywhere and, as a good leader, delegates authority to knowledgeable people in the field of construction. Each attorney has taken the same facts and stated them in a way that is favorable to his or her client.

After the class reviews the trial procedures and the rules for conducting a trial, students are ready to begin their courtroom experience. To begin work on a particular trial, copies of the "Statement of Facts" and all of the affidavits for that trial should be distributed to students.

Please note that in all of the trials except *United States of America v. John Wilkes Booth* and *Lord Capulet v. Friar Laurence*, the state name has been left blank on the official documents. This allows you to add your own choice of state to personalize the trial. In addition, all of the affidavits and the Rental Agreement for *Dale Hampshire v. Clara Muffet* have provisions for a notary public. You can appoint one of the students who is not an attorney to serve in this capacity.

To begin preparation for the trial, read to the class the background information given for that trial. After this, have the students take turns reading the "Statement of Facts" and the affidavits out loud. After the students have a feel for the individuals and issues involved, ask them to select possible roles they might like to take. Having students list at least two choices makes it easier to make the final selections based on the requests and the abilities of the students. Keep in mind that, although it is important to have able attorneys, your witnesses will have to withstand the onslaught of cross-examination and therefore must also be verbally adept.

Once these selections have been made, the two opposing groups will need to prepare for the trial independently in separate locations in the classroom—or, ideally, at separate sites.

Part 3

Trials for Classroom Use

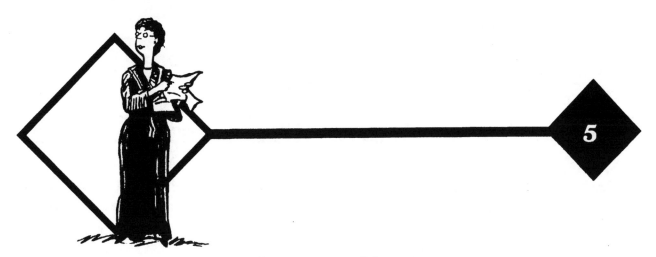

Criminal Trials

Overview

Criminal courts deal with individuals accused of crimes. All crimes are considered offenses against the government in that they violate laws meant to ensure domestic tranquility. The prosecution of such crimes is usually handled by a district attorney or state's attorney. Although the courts are considered a branch of the government, they are a neutral party in trials between the prosecution and the defense.

In the United States, a defendant is presumed innocent until proven guilty. It is the prosecution that bears the burden of proof. The defendant usually retains an attorney to represent his or her interests. Should the defendant be unable to afford such counsel, a court-appointed public defender will ensure that he or she receives legal representation.

Criminal cases are usually tried before a jury that determines whether the accused is guilty or not guilty. The jury can consist of either six or twelve jurors with several alternate jurors sworn in to replace any jury members who are removed before the end of the trial. As stated in the previous chapter, the decision in a criminal trial must be unanimous. The jury must return a "not guilty" verdict if there is a reasonable doubt of the defendant's guilt arising from evidence or lack of evidence.

In the event of a "guilty" verdict, the jury may also be called on to decide the punish-ment, although this is more often determined by the judge presiding over the trial.

The following three trials deal with individuals who have been accused of breaking the law. They have been charged with an assortment of crimes – aggravated battery, criminal mischief, petty theft, and first-degree murder. The principals in each trial will undoubtedly be familiar to your students. As you review the specifics of the trial, make sure that students understand that only the information included in the "Statement of Facts" and the affidavits may be considered as a basis for preparing for trial. Prior knowledge of a different version of the story or historical facts may not be used. The criminal cases that are presented in this section of the book are:

- The State v. Hansel Schmidt and Gretel Schmidt - In this adaptation of the fairy tale *Hansel and Gretel* the youngsters are charged with battery, criminal mischief, and petty theft.

- The State v. Jeremiah Birch - This is an adaptation of the fairy tale *Little Red Riding Hood* in which the neighbor who comes to Hood's aid is charged with aggravated battery.

- The United States v. John Wilkes Booth - Assuming that Booth lived to stand trial, this case charges Booth with murdering President Lincoln.

DOI: 10.4324/9781003236092-5

The State
v.
Hansel Schmidt and Gretel Schmidt

Background Information

In our mock trial version of the fairy tale of Hansel and Gretel, Hansel and Gretel are teenagers who have been abandoned by their father and cruel stepmother in the village of Hexville, which is in Salem County.

After a few days in the small town they decide that if they are going to survive, they must do so on their own. They go into a small bake shop where Hansel claims he is looking for a job so they will have enough money to rent a furnished room and try to live a normal life. The owner of the bakery is Malvinia Crueller, who is famous for her baked gingerbread houses. Indeed, the exterior of her shop is a replica of her famous creations. To attract business, Malvinia has taken on the persona of a witch. She admits she has done this to attract children to her shop.

On entering the shop, Hansel asks Malvinia jokingly if she is really a witch. Apparently she does not see the humor in the question. At this point the account of what happened varies.

According to Malvinia, she observed the two teenagers taking candies and cookies off of her gingerbread houses. When she told them to stop, they refused. She then ordered them out of the shop. They refused and started throwing the baked houses to the floor, breaking them into pieces. When she tried to get them to leave, they fought her. In self-defense, she tried to hit them with a huge baking pan that was in the large oven she used to bake the gingerbread houses. She claims she was no match for the two teenagers and that they tried to push her. When she screamed for help, a neighboring shopkeeper came to her aid. As a result of the struggle she suffered second-degree burns and had to be hospitalized.

Hansel and Gretel dispute Malvinia's version of what happened. They admit they did touch the gingerbread houses but only to admire them. They claim that when Malvinia came after them, one of the houses was knocked to the floor. They say that Malvinia then opened the oven door and pulled out a large pan. She tried to push Gretel into the pan. In the ensuing conflict, several more houses were broken. Hansel and Gretel ran from the shop but realized after running a few blocks that they had no place to go. A police car pulled up and the officer questioned them. They were taken into custody and were later identified in a police lineup by Malvinia Crueller. They are charged with aggravated battery, criminal mischief, and petit theft (petty theft).

Definitions

Aggravated battery - A battery in which a person (1) intentionally or knowingly causes great bodily harm, permanent disability, or permanent disfigurement; or (2) uses a deadly weapon.

Battery - An offensive touching or use of force on a person without the person's consent.

Criminal mischief - An offense involving willfully and maliciously injuring or damaging by any means any real or personal property belonging to another, including, but not limited to, the placement of graffiti thereon or other acts of vandalism thereto.

Larceny - The illegal taking and carrying away of personal property belonging to another with the purpose of depriving the owner of his or her possession.

Petit theft (petty theft) - Larceny of things or goods whose value is below a statutorily set amount that may vary from state to state.

Exhibits

- Plastic bag containing pieces of cookies and candy taken from pockets
- Floor plan of Malvinia's Gingerbread House (optional)

Trial Participants

Prosecution	*Defense*
Attorney(s)	Attorney(s)
Malvinia Crueller	Hansel Schmidt, Defendant
Sammy Snipely	Gretel Schmidt, Defendant
Officer Bertie Johnson	Jackie Horner

Pages 40 - 56 can be reproduced for students and used as beginning documents to present this mock trial.

IN THE CIRCUIT COURT OF THE
THIRTEENTH JUDICIAL CIRCUIT, IN AND
FOR SALEM COUNTY, _____

THE STATE OF _____ ,
  Plaintiff,
-v-
HANSEL SCHMIDT and
GRETEL SCHMIDT,
  Defendants

CASE NO.: 99-666-CF

STATEMENT OF FACTS

At 2 p.m. on October 30, the defendants, Hansel Schmidt and Gretel Schmidt, entered a bakery owned by Malvinia Crueller and operated under the name of Malvinia's Gingerbread House.

Mrs. Crueller asked the defendants if she could be of assistance. They answered that they were just browsing. As there were no other customers in the store, she was able to watch them as they walked about the bakery.

On display were numerous freshly baked gingerbread houses for which the bakery had earned a local reputation. Mrs. Crueller had a large brick oven made especially to accommodate the pans needed to bake the gingerbread houses in one piece. The outside of her establishment resembled a gingerbread house with a facade featuring replicas of the candy and cookies that decorated the baked gingerbread houses.

Mrs. Crueller stated that she observed the defendants picking pieces of candy and cookies from the goods on display. When confronted, they denied the accusation. She asked them to leave the premises. Mrs. Crueller claims that they refused and proceeded to take three of the larger gingerbread houses and smash them on the floor.

A scuffle ensued. In self-defense, Mrs. Crueller opened the door to the oven and tried to pull out a large baking pan. Because she had just completed baking a gingerbread house, the oven was still hot. In the time it took to don her oven mitts, she claims that Hansel Schmidt picked her up and tried to put her in the baking pan. Gretel Schmidt assisted him and tried to close the oven door.

The proprietor of a neighboring shop, Sammy Snipely, heard the commotion and came running to investigate the disturbance. At that time, the defendants ran out of the shop. Snipely assisted Mrs. Crueller and called 911.

The police responded, and Mrs. Crueller was taken to Salem General Hospital and treated for second-degree burns on her arms and hands.

The defendants were apprehended several blocks from the scene. A search revealed pieces of cookies and candy in their pockets. Mrs. Crueller later identified the defendants from a police lineup.

Hansel and Gretel Schmidt claim that it was Mrs. Crueller who attacked them. They assert that after they entered the bakery, she followed them, and as they neared the brick oven, she opened the door, pulled out a large baking pan, and tried to force Gretel into it. During the scuffle, several gingerbread houses were destroyed. They also claim that when they entered the bakery, they had asked in jest if she was really a witch because they had heard rumors to that effect. She said that she had started the rumors herself because of her appearance and that it had been good for business.

After being questioned with their attorney (public defender) present, the defendants were charged with aggravated battery, petit theft (petty theft), and criminal mischief.

IN THE CIRCUIT COURT OF THE
THIRTEENTH JUDICIAL CIRCUIT, IN AND
FOR SALEM COUNTY, _____

THE STATE OF _____ ,
  Plaintiff,
-v-

CASE NO.: 99-666-CF

HANSEL SCHMIDT and
GRETEL SCHMIDT,
  Defendants

GENERAL AFFIDAVIT

_____*Malvinia Crueller*_____ , being first duly sworn according to law, deposes and says that:
       Affiant

I moved to Hexville about seven years ago. After living here about a year, I realized that there was only one bakery in the area, Jackie Horner's Pie Shoppe, and it had a limited selection of baked goods. I decided to open my own shop in my home called Malvinia's Gingerbread House. It, too, would be a specialty shop with homemade gingerbread houses being our biggest seller.

Business was good from the beginning, but I did have problems with some of the children. You know how mean the little dears can be. I am not the prettiest of women, and some of the children said I looked like a witch. One day, I decided that if they thought I looked like a witch, maybe I should start dressing like one. Immediately, word got around that Malvinia Crueller might be a witch. People became curious and came in my shop. Once they tasted my gingerbread specialties, they came again and again.

Sales were so good that I renovated my house so it looked like a gingerbread house. My reputation spread far and wide.

Around 2 p.m. on October 30, two teenagers came into my shop. I later learned their identities to be Hansel and Gretel Schmidt. They were brother and sister. I know from past experience that young people can sometimes be thoughtless. The store was otherwise empty, so I was able to give them my undivided attention. I asked if they needed help, and they said they were just browsing. Apparently to them, browsing meant stealing the candies and cookies from the gingerbread houses on display. When I confronted them, they denied breaking the pieces of candy and cookies off of the houses. You know, if they had asked me, I would have gladly given them a cookie or some of the candy decorations.

I asked them to leave, and they refused. I tried to lead them to the door, but they fought back. Now I'm in good health, but I'm no match for two teenagers. They fought me, and while I was busy with one of them, the other took one of the larger gingerbread houses and smashed it on the floor. As I realized that they could possibly become more violent, I looked for something that I could use to defend myself. I happened to be by one of the large ovens I had installed especially for baking the gingerbread houses in one piece. I opened the door, put on my oven mitts, and went to pick up one of the large pans used for baking the gingerbread houses.

Apparently Hansel saw what I was doing and tried to push me in the oven. When Gretel saw what was happening, she came over and tried to help him. I started screaming, and they ran out of the shop. Fortunately, Sammy Snipely, who owns a neighboring business, heard my cries for help. After helping me out of the oven, he called 911.

I was in the hospital for a week with second-degree burns on my arms and hands. I decided to press charges because I believe that these two young people are a danger to society. In addition to my injuries, the interior of my shop was damaged, and I lost three of my large gingerbread houses.

_____
Affiant

SWORN TO AND SUBSCRIBED before me this _____ day of _____ , in the year _____.

_____
NOTARY PUBLIC
State of _____
My Commission Expires:

IN THE CIRCUIT COURT OF THE
THIRTEENTH JUDICIAL CIRCUIT, IN AND
FOR SALEM COUNTY, _____

THE STATE OF _____ ,
  Plaintiff,
-v-
HANSEL SCHMIDT and
GRETEL SCHMIDT,
  Defendants

CASE NO.: 99-666-CF

GENERAL AFFIDAVIT

___*Sammy Snipely*___ , being first duly sworn according to law, deposes and says that:
Affiant

    I've known Malvinia Crueller ever since she moved here seven years ago. We've never been really friendly, but I admire her. I don't know where she lived before, but she apparently has no family or friends. At least, I've never seen anyone visit her. She approached me about six years ago and wanted to know what I thought of her idea of opening a bakery. I mentioned that Hexville already had Jackie Horner's Pie Shoppe. She said she wanted to open a different kind of shop that would be attractive to children.

    Her business did well in the beginning, but sales really increased after she started dressing like a witch and renovated her house to look like a gingerbread house. Most of her customers were children. There were some adults, but they were few and far between. I never understood why she didn't hire someone to help her. She did all of the baking and selling herself. She did most of the baking late at night. You could smell the gingerbread baking, and occasionally you could smell a roast. I guess she didn't have time to cook her dinner during the day.

    On the afternoon of October 30, a little after 2 p.m., I heard this terrible commotion coming from her store. There was screaming and the noise of metal banging and things crashing around. I ran to her store and was almost knocked over by this teenage boy and girl as they ran out of the store. When I went into the shop, Mrs. Crueller was partway into the oven with her hands and arms resting on a huge baking pan. I helped her out and immediately called 911.

When the police came, I told them what had happened and gave them a description of the two teenagers. I understand they were caught a few blocks away.

It's just terrible. Mrs. Crueller had gone out of her way to make her shop appealing to children. Why, she told me once that she loved children so much she wished she could have them for dinner. I guess she was really lonely.

_____
                                        Affiant

SWORN TO AND SUBSCRIBED before me this _____ day of _____ ,
in the year _____.

_____
NOTARY PUBLIC
State of _____
My Commission Expires:

IN THE CIRCUIT COURT OF THE
THIRTEENTH JUDICIAL CIRCUIT, IN AND
FOR SALEM COUNTY, _____

THE STATE OF _____ ,
  Plaintiff,
-v-
HANSEL SCHMIDT and
GRETEL SCHMIDT,
  Defendants

CASE NO.: 99-666-CF

GENERAL AFFIDAVIT

_____Bertie Johnson_____ , being first duly sworn according to law, deposes and says that:
      Affiant

    I have been a police officer with the Hexville Police Department for 13 years. On October 30 at 2:20 p.m., our office received a 911 call. I was dispatched to 666 Hexville Lane, a commercial establishment operating under the name of Malvinia's Gingerbread House.

    When I entered the bakery, I observed the owner of the bakery, Malvinia Crueller, sitting on the floor next to a large oven. The door to the oven was open, and a large baking pan was resting on it. Mrs. Crueller was being helped by Sammy Snipely, the owner of a neighboring business. Snipely had placed the call to 911. Mrs. Crueller was crying and seemed to be in extreme pain. I called for an ambulance and then asked what had happened.

    Sammy Snipely said there had been a commotion—"screaming, metal banging and things crashing." When running toward the bakery to investigate the disturbance, Snipely claims to have seen a teenage boy and girl leaving the premises. Mrs. Crueller said that they had attacked her and tried to push her into the oven, which was still hot from recent baking. After getting a description from Snipely, I radioed the information, and an All Points Bulletin (APB) was issued.

    Two individuals matching Snipely's description of the teenagers were apprehended about a quarter mile from the scene. They did not offer any resistance and were taken to police headquarters and questioned in the presence of an attorney. They appeared in police lineups and were identified by both Malvinia Crueller and Sammy Snipely as the perpetrators.

I have known Malvinia Crueller since she moved to Hexville seven years ago. In a town as small as ours, the police get to know everyone. She always kept to herself, and we rarely saw her out of her house or business except perhaps when shopping for essential items. She didn't have a car, so I don't know how she got around.

There was talk about her being a witch. Physically, she has fairly irregular features. When one of the kids said she was a witch because she chased him out of her shop, the word spread that she was really a witch. Rather than get upset, she decided to dress the part and always wore black. Business picked up—especially with the children. Adults came in to buy her distinctive gingerbread houses. Her biggest sellers, however, were her gingerbread cookies, which she sold at a reduced price to the children.

The defendants, Hansel and Gretel Schmidt, are new to the area. They can't have been here more than a week. In a town as small as Hexville, I'm sure I'd have been aware of them.

_____
Affiant

SWORN TO AND SUBSCRIBED before me this _____ day of _____ ,

in the year _____ .

_____
NOTARY PUBLIC
State of _____
My Commission Expires:

IN THE CIRCUIT COURT OF THE
THIRTEENTH JUDICIAL CIRCUIT, IN AND
FOR SALEM COUNTY, _____

THE STATE OF _____,
  Plaintiff,
-v-
HANSEL SCHMIDT and
GRETEL SCHMIDT,
  Defendants

CASE NO.: 99-666-CF

GENERAL AFFIDAVIT

Hansel Schmidt , being first duly sworn according to law, deposes and says that:
Affiant

   My sister, Gretel, and I moved to Hexville about a week ago. Actually, we were dropped off here by our father and stepmother. My father is a lumberjack, and business has been very slow. We were on our way to a new place down south where he thought he might be able to find work. About a mile or two out of town, he had a flat tire. Because our luggage was in the trunk on top of the spare, we had to take it out. Gretel and I went to a nearby store to get a soft drink while he fixed the tire. When we came back, our bags were by the side of the road and the car and my father and stepmother were nowhere to be seen.

   Gretel started crying. I had a little money saved from odd jobs I had done, and Gretel had some, too. We've been sleeping in bus shelters and anywhere we could keep warm.

   I soon realized that we were on our own and had to find some way to make money. I met some boys our age and told them we were new in town and that I'd like to get a part-time job. One of them suggested that the witch down the street might be looking for some help. When I asked who the witch was, he pointed to Malvinia's Gingerbread House.

Gretel and I looked at the outside of the shop and then went in. I saw Mrs. Crueller standing in the back and jokingly asked if she was a witch. She just glared at me. She was dressed like one, so I didn't see any harm in asking her. Gretel and I started looking around the shop, and we were really impressed with her gingerbread houses. It was amazing how much they looked like the outside of the shop. She's a real artist. Anyway, I guess we touched one of them when we shouldn't have. She hollered at us and started walking toward us. Gretel got really scared and backed up into one of the houses, and it broke into pieces. Well, that's when Mrs. Crueller really freaked out. She came after us. She put on her oven mitts and opened the big oven door. I thought she was kidding, but then she went after Gretel. I started fighting her, and as a result, more of the gingerbread houses broke. I pushed her, and she landed on the open oven door. I could feel the heat from the oven. There was nothing in it, but it was still very hot. She started screaming, and Gretel and I really got scared. We ran out and saw a man from a neighboring shop running in our direction. We kept running but realized that we had no place to run to. After a few blocks, we slowed down. Gretel was still crying. Then a police car pulled up, and the police took us to the station house. At least we knew we would have a warm place to sleep that night.

I'm really sorry Mrs. Crueller was hurt. I never even got to ask her about the job.

_____
Affiant

SWORN TO AND SUBSCRIBED before me this _____ day of _____ , in the year _____ .

_____
NOTARY PUBLIC
State of _____
My Commission Expires:

IN THE CIRCUIT COURT OF THE
THIRTEENTH JUDICIAL CIRCUIT, IN AND
FOR SALEM COUNTY, _____

THE STATE OF _____ ,
  Plaintiff,
-v-
HANSEL SCHMIDT and
GRETEL SCHMIDT,
  Defendants

CASE NO.: 99-666-CF

GENERAL AFFIDAVIT

_____Gretel Schmidt_____ , being first duly sworn according to law, deposes and says that:
                Affiant

My name is Gretel Schmidt. I'm 14 years old, and my brother, Hansel, is 16. Our mother died about five years ago. I sure do miss her. My father married again a couple of years ago, and our stepmother is really mean. Once she came around, my father didn't pay much attention to us. He's been really upset because business has been very slow. He cuts down trees for lumber mills. Our stepmother kept saying that if they had fewer mouths to feed, they could make ends meet. She said we were old enough to help financially and pay for our own food. I'm sure she talked him into leaving us by the side of the road. He would never do it by himself.

I don't know what I would have done without Hansel. He's really a wonderful big brother. Each of us had some money. Hansel had been cutting lawns and helping our neighbors back home. I had been baby-sitting. Without that money, we would have starved. I'm not old enough to get a regular job, and I know people wouldn't hire me to baby-sit because they didn't know me. We talked it over, and Hansel decided he would get a job and maybe we could get a furnished room someplace. We also wanted to try to go back to school. Hansel met some boys and asked them if they knew where he might get a job. One of them laughingly suggested he ask the witch in Malvinia's Gingerbread House for a job. Now I know why he was laughing.

We went to the shop. The outside of it was beautiful. It looked so real. Each piece of fake candy made me hungry. We went inside and the real ones Mrs. Crueller made looked just like the outside of the shop. She was in the back of the shop when we came in, and we both laughed when we saw her. She really looked like a witch—you know, the kind you see people dress up as on Halloween. Hansel jokingly asked her if she was witch. She didn't think that was funny. We continued walking around the shop looking at the houses and cookies she had made. Everything looked and smelled so good. Anyway, I know we shouldn't have, but we touched one of the houses. She got really upset and came running. She looked at me with this weird look in her eyes. It really scared me. I stumbled and knocked over one of the houses. Candy and cookie pieces were everywhere. Then she really got mad. She put on her oven mitts and opened the oven door to this really big oven. She had this huge baking pan. I never saw one so big. Hansel saw her come after me and started fighting with her to protect me. The two of them were really fighting, and more of the gingerbread houses were broken. Then he gave her a big push, and she landed on the oven door. It must have been hot because she started screaming. Hansel and I ran out of the shop. One of the shopkeepers from a store nearby came running to the bakery as we left.

We kept running for a few blocks, but we didn't know where to go. In a little while, a police car pulled up and took us to the police station. I know I should have been scared, but I felt safe knowing that we had someplace to stay.

_____

Affiant

SWORN TO AND SUBSCRIBED before me this _____ day of _____ , in the year _____.

_____

NOTARY PUBLIC

State of _____

My Commission Expires:

IN THE CIRCUIT COURT OF THE
THIRTEENTH JUDICIAL CIRCUIT, IN AND
FOR SALEM COUNTY, _____

THE STATE OF _____ ,
  Plaintiff,
-v-
HANSEL SCHMIDT and
GRETEL SCHMIDT,
  Defendants

CASE NO.: 99-666-CF

GENERAL AFFIDAVIT

_____Jackie Horner_____ , being first duly sworn according to law, deposes and says that:
        Affiant

    I've owned my own bakery since I was 21. As a little boy I loved pies, so it was just natural for me to go into business making my own. Mine was the only bakery in town until about six or seven years ago. Then Malvinia Crueller opened hers. You might think I'd regard her as competition, but actually we both do a very good business because we sell different types of baked goods.

    I met the defendants a few days before the incident at Malvinia's occurred. They seemed to be new around here. In a town as small as Hexville, everyone knows everyone else. I saw them standing outside of my shop looking at the pies I had on display in my window. As business was slow, I walked outside and started to talk to them. Just being neighborly, you might say. I introduced myself and asked if they were new in town. The boy said his name was Hansel Schmidt and that his sister's name was Gretel. He said they were from up north and that they were just staying in town a few days and passing through. Hansel did most of the talking. He was very polite and referred to me as "sir." Gretel didn't say much. She seemed very shy. I asked where they were staying, and Hansel said he would rather not say.

Around 2:30 p.m. on October 30, I saw them run by the front of my shop. Gretel was crying, and Hansel was telling her to stop. I went outside and looked down the street. They were still running, and then they stopped about a block away. Hansel put his arm around Gretel. He reached in his pocket and gave her something. They stood there talking. I figured everything was all right. So I went back in my shop. Soon I heard an ambulance siren. A little while later, a police car went by my shop with its lights flashing. I went outside to see what was going on. The police car had stopped by Hansel and Gretel. The police officer got out and walked up to them. They talked for a while, and then all three got into the police car.

A little while later, I heard about Malvinia. I don't know who to believe. It always seemed strange to me that she did things to encourage children to come into her shop—you know, like making the outside of the shop look like a gingerbread house and dressing like a witch. Then she got nervous when children came in the shop. I really don't think she would ever hurt a child. She was just afraid they might damage her baked goods. I know how much work goes into baking, so I can understand how she feels.

As for Hansel and Gretel, they seemed to be very polite young people. I think it was probably all a terrible misunderstanding.

_____

Affiant

SWORN TO AND SUBSCRIBED before me this _____ day of _____ , in the year _____ .

_____

NOTARY PUBLIC
State of _____
My Commission Expires:

Formulating Questions for Direct Examination and Cross-Examination

The cases presented in the mock trials in this book are purposely ambiguous. There are no clear-cut solutions. It is up to the attorneys to explore the affidavits for factual weaknesses and inconsistencies. It is important that the attorneys regard all affidavits in this way, not just those of the opposition, so that they can also prepare for cross-examination. The student attorneys should be especially careful to analyze the affidavits to determine which information is factual and which is opinion. *Opinions are only admissible as testimony if offered by an expert witness.* An example would be a DNA expert who could give an opinion as to whether physical evidence at a crime scene matched the DNA pattern of a person accused of the crime.

I have found it best to allow the students to explore their own ideas first. Then ask them specific questions and have them suggest possible ways that both the prosecution and defense might approach each issue. By doing this, the students come to understand that they must look at all aspects of the case from both sides.

Example: Why did Malvinia Crueller encourage children to come into her shop?

Prosecution: She was a lonely old woman who had no children of her own. She had always loved children, and this was her way of compensating for the fact that she had none of her own.

Defense: She was trying to lure them into her shop so that she could do them bodily harm.

You may want to use some of the following questions as guidelines to help students prepare direct and cross-examination questions. Keep in mind that these are only a few areas that could be explored.

1. Why did Malvinia Crueller dress as a witch?

2. Wouldn't it have been more profitable for Malvinia Crueller to try to bring adults into her shop than to encourage children to shop there?

3. If Malvinia Crueller realized that she was no match for two teenagers, why didn't she call the police or someone in the neighborhood for assistance?

4. Could some of Sammy Snipely's testimony have more than one meaning (e.g., "you could smell a roast" and "she loved children so much she wished she could have them for dinner")?

5. Why is Jackie Horner a witness for the defense?

6. Why didn't Hansel and Gretel try to locate their father when they got in trouble?

7. Why didn't Hansel and Gretel try to escape from the police?

8. How did the candy and cookies get into Hansel and Gretel's pockets?

9. If Hansel and Gretel intentionally destroyed the gingerbread houses, what motivated them to do so?

10. Why haven't Hansel and Gretel been seen around town before if the police know everything that is going on in such a small town?

CAUTION: Remind the students that an attorney never asks a question on cross-examination unless he or she knows the answer the witness will give.

IN THE CIRCUIT COURT OF THE
THIRTEENTH JUDICIAL CIRCUIT, IN AND
FOR SALEM COUNTY, _____

THE STATE OF _____ ,
  Plaintiff,

-v-

HANSEL SCHMIDT and
GRETEL SCHMIDT,
  Defendants

CASE NO.: 99-666-CF

JURY BALLOT

_V E R D I C T_

Please circle your choice:

To the charge of aggravated battery, Hansel Schmidt is

    GUILTY   NOT GUILTY

To the charge of criminal mischief, Hansel Schmidt is

    GUILTY   NOT GUILTY

To the charge of petit theft (petty theft), Hansel Schmidt is

    GUILTY   NOT GUILTY

SO SAY WE ALL:

DATED in Hexville, Salem County, _____ , this _____ day of _____ ,
in the year _____ .

_____
Foreperson

IN THE CIRCUIT COURT OF THE
THIRTEENTH JUDICIAL CIRCUIT, IN AND
FOR SALEM COUNTY, _____

THE STATE OF _____ ,
  Plaintiff,
-v-
HANSEL SCHMIDT and
GRETEL SCHMIDT,
  Defendants

CASE NO.: 99-666-CF

JURY BALLOT

V E R D I C T

Please circle your choice:

To the charge of aggravated battery, Gretel Schmidt is

  GUILTY   NOT GUILTY

To the charge of criminal mischief, Gretel Schmidt is

  GUILTY   NOT GUILTY

To the charge of petit theft (petty theft), Gretel Schmidt is

  GUILTY   NOT GUILTY

SO SAY WE ALL:

DATED in Hexville, Salem County, _____ , this _____ day of _____ ,
in the year _____.

_____
Foreperson

The State
v.
Jeremiah Birch

Background Information

This trial combines the essentials of two well-known children's stories and puts a new perspective on the facts.

In this case, Scarlett R. Hood does bring a basket of goodies to her grandma, but this grandma is a modern-day senior citizen, not one to sit home and be waited on. She is active in the local community theater and is in charge of holding auditions for one of the three plays the theater will be presenting this year. This play, *The Master Spy,* requires a male lead who is adept at both male and female disguises. Ivan M. Wolfe, a.k.a. I. M. Wolfe, has gained quite a reputation locally because of a costume he wore last Halloween when he dressed as a sheep.

Mr. Wolfe was unable to attend the regular auditions, so Grandma invited him to her house to try out for the play. After she had given him clothes to effect the disguise, she stepped outside to take her laundry off the clothesline. In the meantime, her granddaughter, Scarlett, entered the house and saw Mr. Wolfe in her grandmother's clothes. In the dim light she sensed something was different about Grandma – her eyes and then her nose. When she recognized that this was a stranger, she screamed. Claiming that he was embarrassed, Wolfe put his hand over her mouth.

Jeremiah Birch, who was in the neighborhood, heard the screams and rushed to Scarlett's rescue. He struggled with Wolfe. According to Birch, he did not know what to expect at Granny's house so he had grabbed an ax from the back of his truck as he ran from his house to her house. This was so he could defend himself and whoever might be in distress.

Unfortunately, Wolfe and Birch had met before this fateful encounter, and they had harsh words at the previous meeting. Birch was close to signing a contract to build a brick house for one of three brothers. Each brother had a house in poor condition; one had been severely damaged in a windstorm. Birch felt that after building the first house, he was sure to get the contracts to build the other two homes. However, a problem arose because the land on which the houses were to be built was owned by Wolfe. Wolfe refused to allow the brick house to be built, saying that he believed Birch wanted to take advantage of the three brothers and that they couldn't really afford such an expensive house. Birch denied this and said that Wolfe wouldn't give permission for the better houses to be built because it would mean an increase in his property taxes. He also asserts that Wolfe did not want to see the brothers improve their living conditions.

Birch allegedly told Wolfe that he would never let Wolfe take advantage of someone again.

Birch has been charged with aggravated battery. His defense states that he injured Wolfe in defense of himself and Scarlett R. Hood.

Definitions

Aggravated battery - A battery in which a person (1) intentionally or knowingly causes great bodily harm, permanent disability, or permanent disfigurement; or (2) uses a deadly weapon.

a.k.a. - An abbreviation meaning "also known as."

Battery - An offensive touching or use of force on a person without the person's consent.

Self-defense - A legal defense that justifies the use of force against another to avoid personal injury or death; this defense is extended to defending others.

Exhibits

- Replica of ax Jeremiah Birch used
- Woman's clothing that I. M. Wolfe was wearing
- Site plan of area around Ada May Moses's house (optional)
- Floor plan of room where Jeremiah Birch and I. M. Wolfe fought (optional)

Trial Participants

Prosecution	*Defense*
Attorney(s)	Attorney(s)
Ada May Moses	Jeremiah Birch, Defendant
Ivan M. Wolfe, a.k.a. I. M. Wolfe	Scarlett R. Hood
Sgt. Terry Hunter	Val Martin

Pages 59 - 75 can be reproduced and used as beginning documents to present this mock trial.

IN THE CIRCUIT COURT OF THE
SECOND JUDICIAL CIRCUIT, IN AND
FOR FORREST COUNTY, _____

THE STATE OF _____ ,
  Plaintiff,
-v-
JEREMIAH BIRCH,
  Defendant

CASE NO.: 98-456-CF

STATEMENT OF FACTS

On May 14 at 4:12 p.m., Sgt. Terry Hunter of the Woodhaven Police Department was called to 364 Maplewood Lane, Woodhaven, to investigate a disturbance. Upon arriving at the scene, he observed a male, later identified as Jeremiah Birch, leaving the residence. This individual approached the police officer and explained that a terrible accident had occurred and someone had been badly hurt.

Sgt. Hunter entered the residence and observed two women bending over a man on the floor. The women were later identified as Mrs. Ada May Moses and her granddaughter, Scarlett R. Hood. The man on the floor, Ivan M. Wolfe, was bleeding profusely from a head wound. Nearby lay an ax with a bloody handle. Sgt. Hunter immediately radioed for an ambulance and backup. Sgt. Hunter used bandages he carried in his car to stem the bleeding from Mr. Wolfe's head. When Birch attempted to aid the officer, Mrs. Moses intervened and shouted, "Don't you dare go near him! You said you were going to get even. Haven't you done enough?"

Her granddaughter, Scarlett R. Hood, replied, "You know that's not true, Grandma. Jeremiah wouldn't hurt anyone. He was just trying to protect you and me from Mr. Wolfe."

After the ambulance and backup patrol came, the victim was removed to a nearby hospital. Surgery, which was required to remove bone fragments from Mr. Wolfe's brain, was pronounced successful. As soon as Mr. Wolfe was well enough to be interrogated, Sgt. Hunter and two detectives from the Woodhaven Police Department questioned him.

Mr. Wolfe said he had gone to visit Mrs. Moses at her invitation. She had asked him to audition for a part in a play in which he was to be a spy who could assume many disguises—both male and female.

Statement of Facts continues on page 60.

He had just donned the disguise of an old woman when Mrs. Moses's granddaughter, Scarlett, arrived with a basket of food her mother had prepared. A few minutes before, Mrs. Moses had stepped outside to take laundry off the clothesline in her backyard because she believed that rain was imminent. When Scarlett came in the house, she recognized her grandmother's clothing but was startled to see that the person wearing the clothing was not her grandmother.

Scarlett became hysterical and began screaming. Suddenly, there was a loud banging at the front door. Then the door burst open, and Jeremiah Birch, a local builder, came in. He saw Mr. Wolfe with his hand over Scarlett's mouth. Mr. Wolfe claims he was trying to calm her down. Mr. Birch and Scarlett claim he was trying to smother her.

A scuffle ensued, and Mr. Birch hit Mr. Wolfe in the head with the handle of the ax he had carried into the house from his truck. Hearing the commotion, Mrs. Moses ran back into the house. Upon viewing Mr. Wolfe with Mr. Birch standing over him with the bloodied ax, she called 911.

Mr. Wolfe claims that this was not the first encounter he had had with Mr. Birch. They had been involved in an argument several weeks before because Mr. Birch was talking to three brothers about building individual houses for them on property owned by Mr. Wolfe. Mr. Wolfe claimed that Mr. Birch was taking unfair advantage of the brothers and had even convinced one of them to build a brick house at a price far beyond his means. Mr. Birch claims that Mr. Wolfe said that even though the places where the brothers lived looked like pigsties, that was all they deserved. Mr. Birch told Mr. Wolfe that it was he who was taking advantage of the three brothers because he knew that if they built better houses on his land, his property taxes would rise.

Mr. Wolfe claims that as he was leaving, Mr. Birch said he would be watching Mr. Wolfe and would make sure that he wouldn't take advantage of anyone ever again. Mr. Wolfe denies taking advantage of anyone and says it was Mr. Birch who wished to take advantage of the three brothers by having them build houses that were too high priced for the area in which they lived.

Mr. Birch claims that the attack on Mr. Wolfe was not premeditated but was rather a defensive act on behalf of an innocent young girl who was being attacked.

After a review of the facts, Jeremiah Birch was charged with aggravated battery. The defense contends that Mr. Birch's actions were in self-defense and defense of another.

IN THE CIRCUIT COURT OF THE
SECOND JUDICIAL CIRCUIT, IN AND
FOR FORREST COUNTY, _____

THE STATE OF _____ ,
  Plaintiff,

-v-

JEREMIAH BIRCH,
  Defendant

CASE NO.: 98-456-CF

GENERAL AFFIDAVIT

_____ *Ada May Moses* _____ , being first duly sworn according to law, deposes and says that:
      Affiant

    I have lived in Woodhaven most of my life. Everyone around here knows me. I must say I have gained quite a reputation in local theatrical circles. Our group, the Woodhaven Players, produces three plays each year. We try to have a musical, a comedy, and a mystery. We are working on our latest production, The Master Spy. I had been looking a long time for the perfect lead. It had to be a man who was strong, agile, and a master of disguise. One of our members said she had heard of a gentleman in a neighboring town by the name of I. M. Wolfe who was creating quite a stir. He apparently had some theatrical background and was adept at assuming various disguises. It was said he could even masquerade as an animal—a sheep, I believe.

    I contacted Mr. Wolfe, but he was unable to attend our auditions because of a previous commitment. I arranged for him to come to my house and audition. He arrived around 3:30 p.m., and after a brief discussion, I gave him some of my clothes and asked him to effect a disguise using them. At about 3:45, my granddaughter, Scarlett, phoned and said she would be over in a few minutes.

    Shortly thereafter, Mr. Wolfe remarked that he thought he heard thunder. I looked outside, and it did appear to be darkening. I had been doing my spring housecleaning, and I had sheets, blankets, and curtains drying on the clothesline. I have a dryer, but I do so like the fresh smell of clothes dried outdoors, don't you? Anyway, I was outside getting the last of the sheets off of the line when I heard screaming and all kinds of commotion.

General Affidavit continues on page 62.

When I went inside, I saw Jeremiah Birch, with a bloody ax in his hand, standing over Mr. Wolfe. He said to Mr. Wolfe, "I warned you that I wouldn't let you take advantage of anyone ever again."

I had spoken to Mr. Birch just the day before. He had come to visit my neighbor, Val Martin, to discuss cutting down some trees for him. Val wasn't home, so Mr. Birch said he would come back another time. He explained he was going to cut down trees to make some extra money because he had just lost a contract to build a brick house. He said he was really upset because he was sure if he built this house, it would lead to contracts to build two other houses. He said that the owner of the land wouldn't allow the tenants to build more expensive houses. Mr. Birch was really upset. He said, "I'd really like to get even with that Ivan Wolfe." I never made the connection that the actor I. M. Wolfe and Ivan Wolfe were one and the same until I saw Mr. Birch standing over him with the ax in his hand.

_____
Affiant

SWORN TO AND SUBSCRIBED before me this _____ day of _____ ,
in the year _____.

_____
NOTARY PUBLIC
State of _____
My Commission Expires:

IN THE CIRCUIT COURT OF THE
SECOND JUDICIAL CIRCUIT, IN AND
FOR FORREST COUNTY, _____

THE STATE OF _____ ,
  Plaintiff,

-v-

JEREMIAH BIRCH,
  Defendant

CASE NO.: 98-456-CF

GENERAL AFFIDAVIT

___Ivan M. Wolfe, a.k.a. I. M. Wolfe___ , being first duly sworn according to law, deposes and says that:
    Affiant

Having just moved to Forrest County a year ago, I bought some inexpensive property I thought I could make a killing on, so to speak. I thought I could make a nice profit on resale in a few years. The people who lived on the land could build their own houses, but the land still belonged to me; therefore, I had to pay the property taxes. The value of the land for tax purposes was based on the types of houses built on it. For the most part, the houses were made out of inexpensive materials, but one of the tenants had fallen victim to an unscrupulous builder, Jeremiah Birch. Birch wanted to build a brick house for him. These people don't have that kind of money. At any rate, Birch and I had words, and he threatened to get even with me because he had lost the contract to build the house.

Last week, I got a call from Mrs. Ada May Moses asking me to audition for a play her theatre group was giving. It sounded like fun. Last Halloween, I had gone to a party dressed as a sheep, and I guess the word got around that I was pretty good at disguises. Anyway, I couldn't make the regular auditions, but Mrs. Moses arranged for me to come to her home to try out. I felt kind of funny when she asked if I could dress as a woman, but when I read the part in the play, I realized that it was very important that the character be able to dress in many different ways. I've always dreamed of going into the theatre, and who knows, someone in the audience might have connections on Broadway or in Hollywood.

Mrs. Moses gave me some of her clothes to try on. The phone rang, and Mrs. Moses answered it. When she hung up, she said that it was her granddaughter, Scarlett, calling to say that she would be over shortly.

General Affidavit continues on page 64.

Then I heard this loud bang. I asked, "Is that thunder?" Mrs. Moses said, "Oh my goodness, I have a line full of sheets and blankets. I can't have them get wet. Why don't you continue working with your disguise while I get the things off of the line?"

She was outside a few minutes when I heard the front door open and close. I was in the living room, which wasn't well lit. I guess there are a lot of trees outside because there was very little light from outside.

I turned around, and there was this lovely young girl. I guessed that this must be Scarlett. She peered at me and said, "Grandma, do you feel all right? Your eyes look very glassy." Before I could say anything, she said, "Grandma, what's the matter with your nose?"

I started to say, "I'm not your grandma," but she started screaming. Now that I look back on it, I guess she had to be startled to see someone else in her grandmother's clothes. The fact that I hadn't shaved made things even worse, I guess. Anyway, she started screaming. I panicked. What would the neighbors think? Suddenly, the door flew open and this huge man entered carrying an ax. I put my hands up in self-defense, but before I knew it, I was on the floor. I must have lost consciousness because the next thing I knew I was in the hospital being readied for surgery.

I later found out it was Jeremiah Birch who attacked me. He said he was going to get even, and I guess he did.

_____

Affiant

SWORN TO AND SUBSCRIBED before me this _____ day of _____ , in the year _____ .

_____

NOTARY PUBLIC

State of _____

My Commission Expires:

IN THE CIRCUIT COURT OF THE
SECOND JUDICIAL CIRCUIT, IN AND
FOR FORREST COUNTY, _____

THE STATE OF _____ ,
  Plaintiff,
-v-
                              CASE NO.: 98-456-CF
JEREMIAH BIRCH,
  Defendant

GENERAL AFFIDAVIT

_____ *Sgt. Terry Hunter* _____ , being first duly sworn according to law, deposes and says that:
        Affiant

    I have been a police officer for the Woodhaven Police Department for the last 20 years. On the afternoon of May 14, I received a call at 4:12 p.m. to investigate a disturbance at 364 Maplewood Lane. I knew the area well and recognized the address as that of Mrs. Ada May Moses. Everyone in town knows her, and ever since her granddaughter was born some years ago, everyone calls her "Grandma Moses."

    When I arrived at the scene, I saw Jeremiah Birch coming out the front door. He was very upset and said there had been a terrible accident. I also know Jeremiah from seeing him around town. When I went into the house to investigate, I saw the victim, a male of undetermined ancestry, lying on the floor. He was wearing women's clothing, something you don't normally see in Woodhaven. It was obvious that he had sustained a severe head wound. He was bleeding profusely and seemed to be in a state of semiconsciousness.

    As I raced back to my car for the first aid kit, I called for backup and an ambulance on my cell phone. I took bandages from the kit and applied them to the wound to try to stem the bleeding. As I applied first aid, Birch came back in the house. Upon seeing him, Mrs. Moses shouted, "Don't you dare go near him! You said you were going to get even. Haven't you done enough?"

    Her granddaughter replied, "You know that's not true, Grandma. Jeremiah wouldn't hurt anyone. He was just trying to protect you and me from Mr. Wolfe."

    Shortly thereafter, two officers in another patrol vehicle arrived, followed by an ambulance. After the paramedics treated the victim, he was taken to Woodhaven Hospital, where I understand he later underwent emergency surgery. Mrs. Moses identified the victim as Ivan M. Wolfe.

General Affidavit continues on page 66.

Under routine questioning, Mrs. Moses told me that Mr. Wolfe was visiting her because she wished to have him audition for a part in a play that required him to be disguised as a woman. This explained why he was wearing women's clothing. She said that about a half hour after he arrived, she received a call from her granddaughter, Scarlett R. Hood, who wanted to make sure her grandmother was home before she stopped by. Shortly after this, Wolfe said he thought he had heard thunder. Mrs. Moses said she hadn't heard it but decided to get her clothes off the line in case it started to rain. As she was doing this, she said she saw Jeremiah Birch drive up in his truck. He got out and started toward the door of her neighbor, Val Martin.

After she had been outside for a few minutes, she heard screaming and yelling coming from the house. She rushed in and saw Jeremiah Birch standing over the victim. An ax with a bloody handle lay nearby. Her granddaughter, Scarlett, was cowering in a corner.

I questioned Scarlett, who said that most of her walk had been in the sun, and when she came into the house, the living room seemed very dark. She then saw an individual whom she believed to be her grandmother. As her eyes became accustomed to the dark room, she said she at first thought that her grandmother was ill because her eyes seemed to be glassy. Then she realized that this individual had a nose that was quite different from her grandmother's. Recognizing that this was not her grandmother, she started screaming.

She said the individual told her to be quiet, and when she didn't stop screaming, he put his hand over her mouth, making it difficult for her to breathe. She said she suddenly heard a loud banging on the door, and it opened and Jeremiah Birch burst in. He had an ax in his hand. A scuffle ensued, and Mr. Birch hit Mr. Wolfe with the ax handle. Scarlett said she didn't believe Mr. Birch had meant to hurt Mr. Wolfe but that he was merely coming to her defense.

When I questioned Mr. Birch, he said he had come to see Val Martin, who lived next door to Mrs. Moses. A few days before, he had met Martin in town and had mentioned that he had lost the contract to build a house. When he said that things were tight financially, Martin asked Birch if he would be interested in earning some money by cutting down trees on the property where Martin lived. Birch said that he had stopped by to check out which trees were to be removed. He had just stepped down from his truck when he heard the screaming from next door. Not knowing what to expect, he grabbed the nearest thing he could use to defend himself—an ax from the bed of his pickup truck.

He said that when he came in the door, Wolfe appeared startled. Birch said he didn't recognize him at first because of his clothing. When he heard Scarlett screaming and saw Wolfe with his hand over her mouth, Birch said he was afraid Wolfe was going to harm her. He said he had dealt with Wolfe and knew he had a bad reputation and liked to take advantage of those who were weaker than him.

_____

Affiant

SWORN TO AND SUBSCRIBED before me this _____ day of _____ ,
in the year _____ .

_____

NOTARY PUBLIC
State of _____
My Commission Expires:

IN THE CIRCUIT COURT OF THE
SECOND JUDICIAL CIRCUIT, IN AND
FOR FORREST COUNTY, _____

THE STATE OF _____ ,
  Plaintiff,
-v-

CASE NO.: 98-456-CF

JEREMIAH BIRCH,
  Defendant

GENERAL AFFIDAVIT

_____*Jeremiah Birch*_____ , being first duly sworn according to law, deposes and says that:
        Affiant

    I have lived in Woodhaven all of my life and know most of the people by sight even if I don't know them personally. I've been trying to start a new business as a builder, but times have been tough. I thought I was finally on my way a few weeks ago after I talked to three brothers who wanted to build better houses on land they rented. One of them was particularly upset because his house had been blown down in a windstorm. He decided that the only thing to do was to build a brick house, which would withstand such calamities.

    I had drawn up the plans when the owner of the land, Ivan M. Wolfe, said the brothers could not build more expensive houses. He claimed that the reason was because they would not get back what they invested in the houses if they were to sell. I know for a fact that he didn't care about them at all. Wolfe told me the places they lived in were no more than pigsties and that was all they deserved. The real reason he didn't want them to build better houses was because he knew the tax assessor would raise his taxes because the value of the property would increase with better houses on it. We argued about this, and I told Wolfe that he liked to take advantage of those who were weaker than he was. I said I was going to watch that he didn't ever do it again.

    About a week later, I met Val Martin in town. We had gone to school together. I told Val about losing the building contract, and it was agreed that I could earn some money by cutting down some trees on Val's property. I went to look over the property on May 13. Val wasn't home, but I spoke to a neighbor, Mrs. Moses. I didn't know her very well but had seen her around town. I did know her granddaughter, Scarlett. She works at the local coffee shop on weekends. Anyway, I told Mrs. Moses about losing the building contract and wanting to earn some money from Val Martin. She suggested that I come back the next day.

As we talked, she told me how excited she was about finding a lead for the play her theatrical group was planning. She said the gentleman was going to audition the following afternoon. She mentioned that his name was I. M. Wolfe, but I never made the connection between him and the Ivan M. Wolfe that I know. He just didn't seem the type to want to act in a play.

The next day, I decided to stop by to see Val again. As I got out of my truck, I heard this terrible screaming coming from Mrs. Moses's house. Not knowing what I would encounter, I looked around for something with which to defend myself. I looked in the back of my truck and saw the ax I had brought with me to cut down any small trees. I knocked on the front door. When there was no answer and the screaming continued, I pushed the door open. I saw Ivan M. Wolfe and Mrs. Moses's granddaughter. She was screaming, and he had his hand over her mouth trying to force her to be quiet. He was wearing women's clothing, and I didn't see Mrs. Moses anywhere. For a moment, I thought the worst: Perhaps he had harmed her and was dressed in her clothes to lure Scarlett into the house. He turned toward me in a threatening manner. We scuffled, and he was much stronger than I had imagined. He also moved very quickly. Not knowing what he might do, I grabbed the ax and struck him over the head with the handle. I just meant to stun him for a minute, but I guess as I came down with the ax handle, he jumped up and hit it. As a result, the force of my blow was increased. I certainly didn't mean to hurt him. I just wanted to stop him from hurting Scarlett. Why, I even offered to help Sgt. Hunter take care of him before the paramedics arrived.

_____

Affiant

SWORN TO AND SUBSCRIBED before me this _____ day of _____ ,

in the year _____.

_____

NOTARY PUBLIC

State of _____

My Commission Expires:

IN THE CIRCUIT COURT OF THE
SECOND JUDICIAL CIRCUIT, IN AND
FOR FORREST COUNTY, _____

THE STATE OF _____ ,
  Plaintiff,

-v-   CASE NO.: 98-456-CF

JEREMIAH BIRCH,
  Defendant

GENERAL AFFIDAVIT

___*Scarlett R. Hood*___ , being first duly sworn according to law, deposes and says that:
Affiant

I've lived in Woodhaven since I was just a few years old. My parents decided to move here to be closer to my grandmother, who lives by herself. My mother really worries about her and is constantly sending over food and things for her. I usually bring them, but if you ask me, I think Grandma can really take care of herself. I always call to make sure she's home before I go over. She's involved in a lot of things here in Woodhaven, especially her theatre group. That's really her favorite project.

I called her around 3:45 p.m. on May 14 to make sure she was home. She didn't tell me she had anyone there, or I would have gone another time. When I got there, I found the front door unlocked, so I figured she had left it open for me. When I walked into her house, it was quite dark. I had forgotten my sunglasses, so the change from the bright outside to her dark house made it hard for me to see.

As I came in, I saw Grandma standing in the living room—at least, I thought it was Grandma. When "she" turned around, I noticed her eyes appeared strange. I asked her if she felt well, but she didn't answer. Then I noticed that her nose appeared enlarged. Suddenly, I realized that this wasn't Grandma but someone dressed in her clothes. I had no idea where she might be. I was very frightened. This person tried to tell me to be quiet, but I started screaming. He put his hand over my mouth, and I had trouble breathing. I continued to scream.

Suddenly, there was a loud banging on the door, and then it burst open. It was Jeremiah Birch. Mr. Wolfe turned toward him, and the two of them started fighting. For a minute I thought Mr. Wolfe was going to hurt Jeremiah. He was very strong. Then Jeremiah picked up an ax, which he had dropped on the floor when he came in the door. He hit Mr. Wolfe with the handle, and Mr. Wolfe fell to the floor with this big gash in his head. There was blood everywhere.

I know Jeremiah from the coffee shop where I work on weekends. He always comes in and tells me about his work. He was really upset because he had recently lost a job that he had been counting on. I told him that he shouldn't let that keep bothering him, but he said he hated to have someone prevent him from getting something for which he had worked so hard. I had no idea that the person who had stopped him from getting the work was Ivan M. Wolfe.

_____

Affiant

SWORN TO AND SUBSCRIBED before me this _____ day of _____ ,

in the year _____.

_____

NOTARY PUBLIC

State of _____

My Commission Expires:

IN THE CIRCUIT COURT OF THE
SECOND JUDICIAL CIRCUIT, IN AND
FOR FORREST COUNTY, _____

THE STATE OF _____ ,
  Plaintiff,

-v-

JEREMIAH BIRCH,
  Defendant

CASE NO.: 98-456-CF

GENERAL AFFIDAVIT

_____*Val Martin*_____ , being first duly sworn according to law, deposes and says that:

Affiant

    I've lived in Woodhaven since I was about six years old. I moved into the house at 360 Maplewood Lane about two years ago. My dry cleaning business has been doing very well, so I decided to buy my first house. The neighborhood is near some woods, and there are many large trees surrounding the houses.

    I have known Jeremiah Birch since high school, and I don't think he has a mean bone in his body. He is not the kind of person to get into a fight, and he has always tried to settle any disagreements in a peaceful manner. He is very active in our peer counseling group and tries to assist those kids who needed help with their self-esteem.

    Things haven't been going too well for him lately. He's been trying to start a construction business. He told me a few weeks ago that he had someone interested in building a brick house to replace an existing house that was in poor repair. If this went well, it might lead to other jobs. The deal fell through, though, when Ivan M. Wolfe, the owner of the land on which the old house was located, wouldn't let Jeremiah build the new brick house.

    Understandably, Jeremiah was upset. I saw him in town, and he told me that not only was he losing a job, but the man who wanted the house built was not going to be able to improve his living conditions. Jeremiah said that this man and his two brothers lived in very poorly constructed houses. Not only were they poorly built, but they were unsafe to live in. Anyone could come and take the little they had and perhaps harm them. Because one of the houses had been damaged in a windstorm, Jeremiah advised the brothers to build the strongest house possible—one made of bricks. He said they were very hardworking men and had saved money to have at least one house built.

The owner of the property, Ivan M. Wolfe, was new to these parts. He apparently was into real estate and really didn't care about people the way Jeremiah does. Jeremiah said Wolfe was the type of person you had to watch out for because he liked to take advantage of people.

Jeremiah and I met at the local coffee shop last week, and I suggested that he could cut down some trees on my property to earn some money until things got better for him. He said he might take me up on the offer. I told him to call me, and we could make an appointment for me to show him what I wanted done.

I was surprised when he showed up on the afternoon of May 14. I guess he was in the neighborhood and decided to stop by. Actually, he never even got to my door. I heard a car pull up and heard a car door shut. I waited for the doorbell to ring, and when it didn't, I figured that it was someone visiting Mrs. Moses next door. It wasn't until a little bit later, when I saw the police car out front and later another police car and an ambulance, that I realized something was wrong.

I still can't believe that Jeremiah would hurt anyone intentionally. He had come by to see about earning some extra money, and now he's being charged with attacking Mr. Wolfe. I'm sure it was self-defense or that Jeremiah was protecting someone else. There's no other explanation.

_____
Affiant

SWORN TO AND SUBSCRIBED before me this _____ day of _____ , in the year _____ .

_____
NOTARY PUBLIC
State of _____
My Commission Expires:

Formulating Questions for Direct Examination and Cross-Examination

You may wish to use the following questions as guidelines to help the students prepare for direct examination and cross-examination. For a fuller discussion of composing questions for witnesses, see page 54 in the mock trial, *The State v. Hansel Schmidt and Gretel Schmidt*.

The following example shows possible approaches by the prosecution and defense to the same question.

Example: Why did Jeremiah Birch tell so many people about losing the contract to build the brick house?

Prosecution: He was very angry and could think of nothing else but getting even with the person who had caused him to lose the job.

Defense: He hoped that if people know he was out of work, they might let him know of any available jobs.

1. Why did Grandma leave a stranger alone in her house while she went outside to take laundry off the line?

2. When Scarlett called, why didn't Grandma tell her she had a guest?

3. Did Ivan M. Wolfe really hear thunder?

4. When did Grandma realize that Ivan M. Wolfe and I. M. Wolfe were the same person?

5. Why did Jeremiah Birch say there had been a terrible "accident"?

6. Why didn't Jeremiah Birch call before he came to visit Val Martin as Martin had asked him to do?

7. How coincidental is it that Jeremiah Birch was visiting Val Martin at the same time that Ivan Wolfe was with Grandma?

8. If Jeremiah Birch really wanted to hurt Ivan Wolfe, why did he only use the handle portion of the ax?

9. Could the increased cost of taxes for Ivan Wolfe's property have been passed on to his tenants, and why wasn't that considered?

CAUTION: Remind the students that an attorney never asks a question on cross-examination unless he or she knows the answer the witness will give.

IN THE CIRCUIT COURT OF THE
SECOND JUDICIAL CIRCUIT, IN AND
FOR FORREST COUNTY, _____

THE STATE OF _____ ,
  Plaintiff,

-v-

JEREMIAH BIRCH,
  Defendant

CASE NO.: 98-456-CF

JURY BALLOT

V E R D I C T

Please circle your choice:

To the charge of aggravated battery, Jeremiah Birch is

    GUILTY   NOT GUILTY

SO SAY WE ALL:

DATED in Woodhaven, Forrest County, _____ , this _____ day of _____ ,
in the year _____ .

_____
Foreperson

The United States of America
v.
John Wilkes Booth

Historical Background

■ Other Presidential Assassinations

Presidential assassins have historically not fared well after committing their heinous crimes.

Charles Julius Guiteau shot **James Garfield** in the back as he was boarding a train in the Washington, D.C., railroad station on July 2, 1881. Garfield lingered, then died September 19, 1881. Some have speculated that his death was due more to unsanitary medical conditions than the gunshot wound. Guiteau was tried for murder and hanged in Washington on June 30, 1882.

Actually, the period of time before Guiteau's execution was longer than Leon Czolgosz, a professed American anarchist. On September 6, 1901, Czolgosz fired two shots at **President William McKinley**, who was holding a public reception at the Pan American Exposition in Buffalo, New York. McKinley died September 14. Czolgosz was speedily brought to trial and sentenced to death September 26. He was executed at the prison in Auburn, New York, on October 29.

Lee Harvey Oswald allegedly shot **President John F. Kennedy** in Dallas, Texas, on November 22, 1963. Oswald never lived to stand trial. He, himself, was assassinated by Jack Ruby, a local nightclub owner.

■ Abraham Lincoln

John Wilkes Booth, a noted Shakespearean actor, shot **President Abraham Lincoln** on April 14, 1865, as he watched a play at Ford's Theater in Washington, D.C. Lincoln died of his wounds the following day. On April 26, Booth was cornered in a barn near Port Royal, Virginia, by a detachment of cal-

vary soldiers. The barn was set on fire, and Booth died of gunshot wounds. Even today, there is some dispute whether the fatal shots were fired from the raiding party or were self-inflicted.

Mary Surratt, Lewis Paine, David Herold (who was captured with Booth in Port Royal), and George Atzerodt stood trial for their role in the conspiracy. They were all found guilty and hanged on July 7, 1865. Dr Samuel Mudd was tried for conspiracy, convicted, and sent to prison. After volunteering to help treat soldiers and prisoners during a yellow fever outbreak, he was pardoned in 1869.

There has been some speculation that the planned assassinations of Lincoln, Vice President Andrew Johnson, and Secretary of State William H. Seward were a conspiracy of someone in the government and not John Wilkes Booth. Secretary of War Edwin Stanton, who played a powerful role following Lincoln's death, was instrumental in the tracking down and attempted capture of John Wilkes Booth. Indeed, wanted posters for John Wilkes Booth, David Herold, and John Surratt, son of Mary Surratt, bore the name of Edwin Stanton as the government official in charge of the investigation. Some have suggested that he may have been the mastermind because he stood to gain a great deal if Lincoln, Johnson, and Seward were eliminated; however, exhaustive investigations over the years have failed to prove this theory.

In reality, John Wilkes Booth died of gunshot wounds during an attempt to capture him in a barn in Port Royal, Virginia. ***For our mock trial purposes, we have hypothesized that Booth was captured and lived to stand trial.***

Background Information

The defendant, John Wilkes Booth, had long carried a hatred for the North. The focus of his hatred was President Abraham Lincoln. He stated that the president was tyrannical and evil. When Lincoln was elected to his second term, it is believed that Booth's hatred reached a boiling point. He plotted to kidnap the president and hold him until Southern prisoners were released from the Northern prison camps. During the early part of 1865, Booth met with several men to plot the abduction. Among these co-conspirators was George Atzerodt, who had experience as a blockade runner, breaking through the blockade the North had set up to cripple the South. He was to supply a boat that could be used to spirit Lincoln away and hide him until an agreement could be reached. Other conspirators included Lewis Paine, David Herold, and John Surratt. They met frequently at the boardinghouse of John Surratt's mother, Mary Surratt. Michael O'Laughlin and Sam Arnold were also members of the group but refused to participate in the final assassination plans.

Several attempts at kidnapping the president failed. According to Atzerodt and Paine, Booth became increasingly agitated and changed the plan from kidnapping to murdering the president, Vice President Andrew Johnson, and Secretary of State William H. Seward. Booth was going to personally assassinate president Lincoln, Paine was to murder Seward, and Atzerodt was assigned to kill Johnson. Booth claimed that he was receiving orders from a higher source and that instructions were changed when the kidnapping attempts failed.

Booth was successful in assassinating Lincoln. Paine attacked Seward with a knife, but the wounds did not prove to be fatal. Atzerodt, however, wanted no part of murder. He claimed he was willing to assist in the abduction of the president but unwilling to kill Johnson. On that fateful night of April 14, 1865, Atzerodt opted to get drunk and go into hiding.

Earlier in the day, John Wilkes Booth visited Ford's Theater to lay the groundwork for killing the president. He inspected the presidential box and watched the actors rehearsing *Our American Cousin*. As he listened to the actors reciting the lines of the play, with which he was familiar, he estimated the most opportune time for the attack. He also planned his escape, from the dramatic leap onto the stage after the shooting of the president to the horse waiting for him to make his getaway.

The presidential party was delayed and arrived after *Our American Cousin* had begun. The play was halted, and "Hail to the Chief" and cheers from the audience greeted the president. The play resumed, and shortly thereafter, presidential guard Detective John F. Parker left his post to go to a local tavern for a pint of ale. There he observed Booth, who had dropped in and ordered a bottle of whiskey and water. A patron in the tavern taunted Booth, telling him he would never be the actor his father was. Booth rightly prophesied that when he left the stage he would be the most famous actor in America.

Booth returned to Ford's Theater and entered the unguarded presidential box. He shot Mr. Lincoln and, in a scuffle, stabbed Major Henry Reed Rathbone, a member of the presidential party who came to the president's aid. Booth then attempted his dramatic leap onto the stage but caught his foot on the flag draping the theater box. He fell to the stage, breaking his leg. Despite his injury, he reached his horse and escaped.

As had been prearranged, he met David Herold, who was to assist him in his escape.

They rode through the night, soon realizing that Booth was going to need medical aid. They arrived at the home of Dr. Samuel Mudd around 4 a.m. Booth had met Mudd some months before when the two had discussed some land that Dr. Mudd had for sale. Booth had a scarf drawn around his face, and in the dim lamplight, Mudd did not recognize him. Herold stated that his friend, a "Mr. Tyson," had fallen from his horse and hurt his leg. Dr. Mudd treated the leg, and Herold and Booth went on their way.

On April 26, 1865, a detachment of calvary officers in the charge of Lieutenant Edward Doherty surrounded a barn belonging to Richard Garrett near Port Royal, Virginia. They placed John Wilkes Booth under arrest. (In reality, Booth died of a gunshot wound in the barn. There is some question whether he was shot by an army officer or whether he shot himself.)

Once again, recall that for our mock trial purposes, Booth has been indicted for first-degree murder and treason and a trial date set.

Incidences described in the affidavits were based on actual events detailed in materials about the assassination of Abraham Lincoln, about John Wilkes Booth, and about other individuals involved in the conspiracy to kill the president and other high government officials. Certain facts have been changed or embellished for mock trial purposes. The changed facts are:

1. John Wilkes Booth did not live to stand trial.

2. Laura Keene's affidavit gives a possible insight she may have had, since she was a stage actress for a long time and came in frequent contact with the Booth family.

3. The insanity defense might not have been used at this time in history, but it is known that judgments were made about individuals based on their mental state. As an example, 10 years after President Lincoln's death, his widow, Mary Todd Lincoln, was certified as a "lunatic" and committed to an institution, where she remained for a year.

Definitions

First-degree murder - A homicide that is willful, premeditated, and deliberate.

Insanity defense - A plea acknowledging the commission of the crime but asserting that there was no criminal intent because the defendant suffered from a defect of mind in which he or she did not understand the nature of the act or did not know that it was wrong; the defense is required to show that insanity prevented the requisite mens rea from being formed.

Mens rea - Guilty mind; the state of mind required to be held criminally liable for an act.

Treason - The offense of attempting by overt acts to overthrow the government of the state to which the offender owes allegiance or to kill or personally injure the head of state.

Exhibits

- Replica of one-shot derringer
- Map of route Booth took before his capture (optional)
- Floor plan of Ford's Theater (optional)

Trial Participants

Prosecution	*Defense*
Attorney(s)	Attorney(s)
George Atzerodt	John Wilkes Booth, Defendant
Detective John F. Parker	Edwin Booth
Clara Harris	Dr Samuel Mudd
Mary Surratt	Laura Keene

(It is strongly suggested, that because of the complexity of this trial, each side should have more than one attorney.)

Pages 80 - 99 can be reproduced and used as beginning documents to present this mock trial.

IN THE UNITED STATES
DISTRICT COURT
FOR THE DISTRICT OF COLUMBIA

THE UNITED STATES OF AMERICA,
  Plaintiff,
-v-
JOHN WILKES BOOTH,
  Defendant

CASE NO.: 65-13-CF

STATEMENT OF FACTS

On the evening of April 14, 1865, U.S. President Abraham Lincoln was shot with a one-shot derringer pistol at Ford's Theatre at Tenth Street, Washington, D.C. The following morning, he died of his wounds. John Wilkes Booth, a noted Shakespearean actor, has been charged with the crime and with masterminding a plot to kill Vice President Andrew Johnson and Secretary of State William H. Seward.

Booth admits that he pulled the trigger of the gun, killing the president, but denies masterminding the plan for the killing. He claims that he had received orders from an unknown source and that others, who were committed to the cause of the South and believed that Lincoln had to be eliminated, were the ones who had planned the assassinations of the president, vice president, and secretary of state.

Booth, who was a familiar face in the theatre, had no difficulty gaining entry to the area where the presidential box was located. Detective John F. Parker, who was assigned to protect the president, had left to go to a local tavern. There was no guard on duty outside the box. After shooting the president and stabbing Major Henry Reed Rathbone, who was viewing the play with the president, Booth jumped from the box onto the stage, shouting, "Sic semper tyrannis!" ("Thus always to tyrants.") He then made his getaway on a horse that was being cared for by a stableboy outside the back entrance to the theatre.

On Wednesday, April 26, 1865, a detachment of cavalry officers in the charge of Lieutenant Edward Doherty surrounded a barn belonging to Richard Garrett near Port Royal, Virginia. They placed John Wilkes Booth under arrest for the assassination of the president. Also arrested at this time was David Herold, an alleged accomplice.

John Wilkes Booth has been indicted for first-degree murder and treason. The one-shot derringer pistol used in the assassination has been recovered.

Booth stated that the original plan was to kidnap President Lincoln and hold him hostage in exchange for Confederate prisoners being held by the North. When several kidnap attempts failed, the decision was made to kill the president, Vice President Andrew Johnson, and Secretary of State William H. Seward. Booth stated that the only way the country could be free of the evil Lincoln was to get rid of him permanently.

The defense asserts that John Wilkes Booth has a history of bizarre behavior and has shown indications of insanity, believed to be inherited from his father, Junius Brutus Booth. Throughout his theatrical career, John Wilkes Booth had been constantly reminded that he was not the actor that his father was or as great as his brother, Edwin Booth, who was famous worldwide for his portrayal of Hamlet. The defense states that John Wilkes Booth's motive was to make sure that his name would go down in history even if it meant killing the president of the United States. The defense claims that the combined reelection of Lincoln, defeat of the South, and inability of Booth to live up to the worldwide reputations of his father and brother caused John Wilkes Booth to snap. They further state that some prominent government officials were aware of Booth's weaknesses and used him as a means to further their own plans to gain control of the country. They are entering a plea of not guilty by reason of insanity.

IN THE UNITED STATES
DISTRICT COURT
FOR THE DISTRICT OF COLUMBIA

THE UNITED STATES OF AMERICA,
  Plaintiff,
-v-
JOHN WILKES BOOTH,
  Defendant

CASE NO.: 65-13-CF

GENERAL AFFIDAVIT

_____*George Atzerodt*_____, being first duly sworn according to law, deposes and says that:
          Affiant

I am a carriage maker from Port Tobacco, Virginia. Sometimes people call me "Port Tobacco." During the war, I worked as a blockade runner, and I guess I acquired quite a reputation. David Herold brought John Wilkes Booth to me in Port Tobacco because he knew I sympathized with the cause of the Confederacy. I also made a pretty penny breaking through the blockade the Union had set up to cripple the South economically.

Booth talked about a plot to kidnap President Lincoln and hold him hostage until an agreement could be made to release Southern prisoners from prison camps in the North. I had heard the conditions in these camps were terrible. I wanted to do what I could to help set these prisoners free, so I told them I knew of a boat we could use to take the president away after he had been kidnapped.

After this, a group of us met at Mrs. Surratt's boardinghouse several times to discuss the plan. There were seven or eight of us willing to work with Booth. There, I met Lewis Paine and Mrs. Surratt's son, John.

I was willing to help with this plan because I felt the president would only be kidnapped, not harmed. We tried to kidnap the president several times, but each time something happened to prevent us from taking him. The group started to fall apart. The only ones left were David Herold, Lewis Paine, Booth, and me.

Then Booth told us the plan had been changed. It was going to be much bigger, and the president and others were going to be killed. The plan was for Booth to kill the president and Paine to murder Secretary of State Seward. I was supposed to kill Vice President Johnson. I felt sick. There was no harm in kidnapping the president, but I had not bargained for murder. I guess I was the only one who felt that way. Lewis Paine didn't say anything when Booth outlined his new plan. As for David Herold, he looked at Booth as if he were God. I guess Booth must have seen the look on my face because he said that anyone who didn't go along with the plan should be shot.

I was really upset about the new plan. I started to drink heavily. I didn't like this at all. I tried to block the terrible plan from my mind.

The day before our plan was to take place, Booth had me register at the Kirkwood House. Vice President Johnson was staying there. I rented a room on the floor above his. There, I was supposed to follow his movements.

The final plan was for the three assassinations of Lincoln, Johnson, and Seward to take place around 10:15 p.m. on April 14. I couldn't do it. I checked up on Mr. Johnson, and he seemed to be a nice man. I may be a drinker, but I'm not a killer. I wandered around that night and for a few days after until the police captured me.

Blockade running may have been illegal, but it was nothing compared to this mess.

_____
                                                Affiant

SWORN TO AND SUBSCRIBED before me this _____ day of _____ , in the year _____ .

_____
NOTARY PUBLIC
State of _____
My Commission Expires:

IN THE UNITED STATES
DISTRICT COURT
FOR THE DISTRICT OF COLUMBIA

THE UNITED STATES OF AMERICA,
  Plaintiff,

-v-

JOHN WILKES BOOTH,
  Defendant

CASE NO.: 65-13-CF

GENERAL AFFIDAVIT

_____*John F. Parker*_____ , being first duly sworn according to law, deposes and says that:
            Affiant

    I was a member of a four-man special police force assigned to defend the president. Mrs. Lincoln herself had purposely written a letter requesting that Joe Sheldon and I should be on the force. Of course, this meant that we could not serve in the Army, but we felt it a great honor and duty to serve the president. Prior to this, I had served in the Union forces for three months. In 1861, I was accepted as a member of the Washington, D.C., police force. At times I had disagreements with my superiors because but I felt that they were a bit demanding.

    On the night of April 14, 1865, I was assigned to protect the president. My shift began at 4 p.m., when I was supposed to replace Officer William Crook. Unfortunately, I was delayed. I took over at 7 p.m. Crook informed me that the president, Mrs. Lincoln, Major Henry Rathbone, and his fiancée, Miss Clara Harris, were going to Ford's Theatre that evening. As there was no room in the coach, I was to leave the White House 15 minutes early and meet the presidential party at the theatre.

    I went into the theatre and thoroughly checked the box the presidential group was to occupy. Everything seemed to be in order. Soon after, the carriage arrived from the White House. After all of its occupants were safely out of the carriage, I led them to their seats. The play, which was already in progress, was halted, and the audience applauded as the president and his party were seated. I felt secure knowing that Major Henry Reed Rathbone, a distinguished Army officer, was with the president. I had also seen two Army officers take the last two seats in Row D just before the curtain rose. I felt the president was well protected.

I returned to my post, but I could not see the play. The evening was beginning to drag, and I was very thirsty. Because I knew the president and first lady were safe, I saw no reason why I couldn't go to Taltavul's, a little tavern down the street, for a bit of ale. There I met Burns, the presidential coachman, and Forbes, the president's valet.

After a few drinks, we looked up to see a new arrival. John Wilkes Booth had stopped in. He asked for a bottle of whiskey and water. He appeared very calm. Not a bit nervous. Then one of the drunks at the bar began taunting Booth. He said, "You'll never be the actor your father was."

Booth wasn't upset at all. He just smiled and said, "When I leave the stage, I will be the most famous man in America."

A lady friend of mine stopped by. Because I knew the president was well protected, I decided to spend some time with her. I didn't find out what had happened until later. There is no way the tragedy could have been prevented. Why, the president had an Army man in the box with him and two Army men in the audience. Even Major A. C. Richard, superintendent of the Washington police force, was in the audience.

_____
Affiant

SWORN TO AND SUBSCRIBED before me this _____ day of _____ ,
in the year _____ .

_____
NOTARY PUBLIC
State of _____
My Commission Expires:

IN THE UNITED STATES
DISTRICT COURT
FOR THE DISTRICT OF COLUMBIA

THE UNITED STATES OF AMERICA,
  Plaintiff,

-v-

CASE NO.: 65-13-CF

JOHN WILKES BOOTH,
  Defendant

GENERAL AFFIDAVIT

_____*Clara Harris*_____ , being first duly sworn according to law, deposes and says that:
                     Affiant

Major Henry Reed Rathbone, my fiancé, and I had received a last-minute invitation to attend a performance of <u>Our American Cousin</u> at Ford's Theatre with President and Mrs. Lincoln. Although many have declined invitations from them, we were delighted to join them. It's true that Mrs. Lincoln does behave strangely at times, but, in general, we enjoy her company.

We arrived late because the president had a last-minute meeting. The crowd gave its usual enthusiastic greeting for the president they all loved so dearly. We sat down to enjoy the play. The president was seated in a rocking chair, which was kept there especially for him. Mrs. Lincoln sat to his right on a cane chair. The president's valet, Forbes, came in with us but left after a short while. Henry, who wasn't in uniform, was seated on a sofa about 7 feet to the president's right—away from the entrance to the box. I was seated near him.

It was the second scene of Act III, and Harry Hawks, the lead actor, had just said something terribly funny. The audience laughed. At the same time, I heard a noise, which I later realized was a gunshot. There was a cloud of smoke in the box. Henry leaped to his feet. He quickly realized that the president had been shot, and he attacked the assailant. This was a brave thing to do as Henry was unarmed. The man had a knife and attacked Henry. They struggled, and Henry's arm was cut badly. The man shouted "Revenge for the South" and jumped from the box onto the stage.

I don't know what happened to him after that. I screamed for help and water. Henry was bleeding profusely, the president was slumped in his chair, and Mrs. Lincoln was crying, "They've killed him!" It was just terrible.

How Mr. Booth got into that box I don't know. There was a guard outside. Mr. Booth could not have been in the box long before he shot the president. Henry or I would have seen him. Booth had a gun and a knife. Henry said Booth knew he would not have time to reload his one-shot derringer. He had a knife to use after firing the gun's single bullet.

_____
Affiant

SWORN TO AND SUBSCRIBED before me this _____ day of _____ ,
in the year _____.

_____
NOTARY PUBLIC
State of _____
My Commission Expires:

IN THE UNITED STATES
DISTRICT COURT
FOR THE DISTRICT OF COLUMBIA

THE UNITED STATES OF AMERICA,
  Plaintiff,
-v-

CASE NO.: 65-13-CF

JOHN WILKES BOOTH,
  Defendant

GENERAL AFFIDAVIT

_____*Mary Surratt*_____, being first duly sworn according to law, deposes and says that:
  Affiant

I own a boardinghouse at 541 H Street, Washington, D.C. I opened it two years ago after my husband died. We had a farm, and my husband was postmaster in Surrattsville, Maryland, until his death. I tried to keep it up, but it was too difficult. I decided to rent it out and bought the boardinghouse. It was to be the new home for my three children: Isaac, who was a rider for the Pony Express and a Confederate soldier; John, who had left the seminary and was a Confederate courier; and, of course, my daughter, Anna. The money we got from it was going to keep us from starving. Our tenant at the farm was often late with his rent.

John sometimes had his friends over. When I asked him why these men were coming to the house at such odd hours, he said they were all interested in common oil speculation. Occasionally, Mr. John Wilkes Booth would visit, and these were special times. Of course, my daughter, Anna, was as thrilled as you can imagine any 17-year-old girl might be if a famous actor visited. But I noticed that whenever Mr. Booth came, the other members of John's group were all there and very serious. These members would include George Atzerodt, David Herold, Lewis Paine, Michael O'Laughlin, and Sam Arnold.

I knew Mr. Booth traveled a great deal as an actor, and I figured he always brought new information with him about the oil deals.

The last time I saw my son John was at the end of March when he left for Richmond to see if he could get a clerkship.

On April 11, I went to Surrattsville to collect $479 that Mr. John Nothey had owed me. He had purchased 75 acres of farmland from my husband many years ago and had never paid him for it. My financial situation was very tight since my son John had left, and I decided to go to Mr. Nothey and try to collect the money.

Mr. Booth heard where I was going and asked me to deliver a message. I was supposed to stop and see a Mr. John Lloyd and give him the message, "Have the things ready to be picked up." The police are trying to say that the message was "Have the guns ready to be picked up" and that I was part of the conspiracy to kill the president.

I may not have always agreed with Mr. Lincoln, but I certainly wouldn't have anything to do with killing him. I'm a fine Catholic woman. I went to church on Good Friday, the day he was killed. Do you think I could go to church during the day and help to plan a murder at night?

Mr. Booth used his charm and fine acting ability to persuade those young men to go along with his plan. John must have known what was happening. I guess that's why he left.

_____

Affiant

SWORN TO AND SUBSCRIBED before me this _____ day of _____ ,

in the year _____.

_____

NOTARY PUBLIC

State of _____

My Commission Expires:

IN THE UNITED STATES
DISTRICT COURT
FOR THE DISTRICT OF COLUMBIA

THE UNITED STATES OF AMERICA,
  Plaintiff,

-v-

JOHN WILKES BOOTH,
  Defendant

CASE NO.: 65-13-CF

GENERAL AFFIDAVIT

_____*John Wilkes Booth*_____ , being first duly sworn according to law, deposes and says that:
          Affiant

    I am one of a family of actors, known throughout the world. I have appeared on the stage in many different kinds of plays, ranging from light comedy to the tragedies of Shakespeare. In addition to me, my father, Junius, and my brother, Edwin, are also world famous.

    I have performed throughout the North and South. When I traveled in the South, I could not help but be moved by the plight of the Southern plantation owners. They had spent their lives building their land with the help of their Negro slaves. Then that tyrant Lincoln came along and said that the Negroes were as good as the White man and that they should be free—free to live wherever they want and work wherever they want like the White man. Can you imagine that? Everyone knows that this great United States was founded for the White man. Why, many of the men who wrote the Constitution had slaves. Everyone knows that when they said that all men are created equal, they didn't mean slaves.

    Many of our fine Southern boys were killed defending their rights. We can never bring them back. Many more were being held prisoner in the North. Our generals tried to negotiate an exchange of prisoners—Yankees for Southern lads—but General Ulysses S. Grant (obviously under the orders of his commander in chief) refused repeatedly. Our boys were left to rot in Northern prisons. Because of how I felt about the Southern cause, I was contacted through a messenger to see if I would like to help get our boys back. The plan was to kidnap Mr. Lincoln and exchange him for our prisoners. That Yankee monster perpetrated this evil upon the South when he signed the Emancipation Proclamation on January 1, 1863, proclaiming the freedom of all slaves in the South and then absolute freedom of all Negroes in the North and South earlier this year. Perhaps if we had the president in our hands, we would have a chance to free our Southern boys.

We tried many times to kidnap the president. Each time, we failed. One time, he didn't show up when he was supposed to appear at a play. Another time, he was not in a carriage that we had believed he would be in. Another time, he was ill. It was as if the devil himself was helping him to escape. Our original plan on the night of April 14 was to tie up the president, and after turning down the gaslights in Ford's Theatre, lower him onto the stage and escape with him in a waiting carriage. Surely, the world would be more aware of our cause if we made such a daring capture!

On the morning of April 13, my orders were changed. Evidently, it was realized that the only way to stop the evil that this man had created was to do away with him and the others who were responsible for making a shambles of our fine Southern traditions. It was our responsibility to snatch victory from defeat, to determine with our own hands whether the South lived or died. That traitor from Tennessee, Johnson, also had to die. He would only continue what Lincoln had started. Secretary of State Seward was sure to guide him. He had to be eliminated too.

You've got to understand. We had no choice. When I fired the bullet that killed that tyrant, I felt that I had freed the South from the tyrannical bonds that the North had placed upon it. It was my duty to save the South and its way of life from the forces of tyranny and oppression. Our country owed all her troubles to him, and God simply made me the instrument of his punishment.

My father, Junius Brutus Booth, was known as a great tragedian, and my brother, Edwin, was famous for his Hamlet, but years from now, who will be the most famous Booth of all? I, John Wilkes Booth, will be remembered as the one who played the greatest role of all time—far greater than any Shakespeare had to offer.

_____
Affiant

SWORN TO AND SUBSCRIBED before me this _____ day of _____ ,
in the year _____.

_____
NOTARY PUBLIC
State of _____
My Commission Expires:

IN THE UNITED STATES
DISTRICT COURT
FOR THE DISTRICT OF COLUMBIA

THE UNITED STATES OF AMERICA,
 Plaintiff,
-v-

CASE NO.: 65-13-CF

JOHN WILKES BOOTH,
 Defendant

GENERAL AFFIDAVIT

_____*Edwin Booth*_____, being first duly sworn according to law, deposes and says that:
            Affiant

   I was five years old when my brother, John Wilkes Booth, was born in Hartford County, Maryland. Our family life revolved around the stage. My father, Junius Brutus Booth, was widely regarded as the finest Shakespearean actor of all time. I traveled with him throughout the United States and Australia until his death in 1852.

   Unfortunately, as great an actor as my father was, he often suffered bouts of insanity. These usually occurred after he had been drinking heavily. He also studied various religions and believed that when someone died he would come back in another life time as an animal. If we had a bird die near our house, Father would insist on having full funeral services and burial for it.

   I often thought that John had inherited some of my father's insanity. One time, when John was angry, he killed a mother cat and her litter of kittens. Father wept uncontrollably. Another time, John had a horse pull him on a sleigh into town and back to win a bet. This incident occurred in the middle of summer. Can you imagine a horse pulling a sleigh in summertime?

   One time during a performance of Richard III, a fellow actor fled from the stage convinced that John was really trying to kill him. Another time, during Othello, the actress playing Desdemona said that John was actually trying to use a pillow to smother her.

   John was often upset because he never received the rave reviews that Father or I received after our Shakespearean performances. In fact, early in his career, the audience often hissed because of his poor performance. He is still rather young, 26 years old, and I believe that, given time, he could have developed into a great actor.

The last time I saw him, a few weeks before the killing of the president, he told me he was playing the greatest role of his life. He said he was living it every day. I thought nothing of it, as actors often take on the actions and moods of a character when they are preparing for a role.

He did not mention his plan to harm the president, but I would not have expected him to do so. We have always disagreed on politics. He had always strongly supported the Confederacy, and he knew I felt equally as strong about the North.

I love my brother. He had said his name would go down in history and that he would be the most famous Booth of all. I was shocked when I heard about his terrible deed. John was acting out a role, the greatest of his life. He was going to satisfy his need to be more famous than his father or me.

_____
Affiant

SWORN TO AND SUBSCRIBED before me this _____ **day of** _____ ,
in the year _____.

_____
NOTARY PUBLIC
State of _____
My Commission Expires:

IN THE UNITED STATES
DISTRICT COURT
FOR THE DISTRICT OF COLUMBIA

THE UNITED STATES OF AMERICA,
  Plaintiff,
-v-

CASE NO.: 65-13-CF

JOHN WILKES BOOTH,
  Defendant

GENERAL AFFIDAVIT

_____*Dr. Samuel Mudd*_____ , being first duly sworn according to law, deposes and says that:
       Affiant

I first met John Wilkes Booth in December of 1863. I own a lot of good property between Bryantown and Waldorf, Maryland. He asked me about land, but when I told him about some good parcels, he seemed more interested in land on good roads. I invited him to spend the night. As it turned out, he did not purchase land but did buy two horses from a friend of mine.

In our conversations, Mr. Booth was most sympathetic to my plight. I owned seven slaves, and Union General Winfield Scott was making wholesale arrests without formal charges of anyone he suspected of being disloyal to the Union. There were more than 20,000 federal troops in Charles County alone. I was afraid.

Mr. Booth and I talked about what had happened to the once proud and gentle South. He felt that the president was to blame and that if he was going to serve another four years in office, our entire country would be in a very sad state. I had to agree with him in some areas, but he seemed to be obsessed with hatred for Mr. Lincoln. He was wild-eyed and ranted about "that tyrant Lincoln." I saw similar mannerisms in patients in mental institutions when I practiced medicine some years ago.

I saw Mr. Booth fleetingly on various occasions over the next few months but had little occasion to talk to him. We merely exchanged pleasantries.

Then around 4 a.m. on the morning of April 15, there was a loud knocking on my door. When I opened it, a stranger appeared and said his companion had had a riding accident and hurt his leg badly. I had him bring his friend into the house. His friend was wrapped in a heavy coat and had a huge scarf around his face. In the dim candlelight, I could only see his eyes and cheekbones. He was in a great deal of pain. He did not remove the scarf, and I assumed that perhaps he was in mild shock from his injury. I set the leg, which had a simple fracture of the tibia and no fracture of adjoining bones. I had to cut the boot off to reach the injured area.

Later on, the uninjured man came down from the bedroom where his friend was resting. He said his name was Henston and the injured man was Mr. Tyson. He asked if I had a razor to lend his friend. While I was setting the fracture, the scarf had slipped from his friend's face. I noted a full gray beard and a black mustache. I thought it unusual that someone would choose at this time to shave a beard that must have taken such a long time to grow.

I did not suspect that I might have treated Mr. Booth until I heard the news later in the day about the president's assassination.

As a physician, I would still have treated Mr. Booth if I had to do it all over again. I took an oath to help the injured and sick. Mr. Booth was sick, not only in body but in mind.

_____

Affiant

SWORN TO AND SUBSCRIBED before me this _____ day of _____ ,

in the year _____.

_____

NOTARY PUBLIC

State of _____

My Commission Expires:

IN THE UNITED STATES
DISTRICT COURT
FOR THE DISTRICT OF COLUMBIA

THE UNITED STATES OF AMERICA,
  Plaintiff,

-v-

CASE NO.: 65-13-CF

JOHN WILKES BOOTH,
  Defendant

GENERAL AFFIDAVIT

_____*Laura Keene*_____ , being first duly sworn according to law, deposes and says that:
      Affiant

My name is Laura Keene, and I am an actress by profession. On that terrible night, Friday, April 14, I was starring in Our American Cousin, in a role I must have played a thousand times. It was the first night of our run at Ford's Theatre, and we expected a light turnout as it was Good Friday. We were delighted when we heard early in the day that President and Mrs. Lincoln would be attending that evening's performance. Signs were posted outside the theatre.

We were rehearsing that morning when I saw John Wilkes Booth wandering around the theatre. This was not unusual as actors frequently come to theatres when they are not acting, just to be around other actors and the atmosphere.

That evening, we waited for the president and first lady to arrive. After a short time, we decided to begin the play, as the Lincolns had in the past said they would come to a play and then changed their minds at the last minute. We were into the second act when they arrived. Immediately, the play stopped, and the orchestra began playing "Hail to the Chief." The crowd cheered, and the presidential party was seated in the box immediately above the stage. Mrs. Lincoln seemed to enjoy the play, laughing frequently, but Mr. Lincoln was quiet and seemed tired.

We were in the second scene of the third act. Harry Hawk was on the stage alone. I was waiting to go on. The stage manager and two stagehands were storing scenery. Harry had just said his funniest line of the play, "Don't know the manners of good society, eh? Well, I guess I know enough to turn you inside out, you sockdologizing old man trap!" The audience roared with laughter.

Suddenly there was a great deal of commotion in the presidential box. The president was slumped over, and Mrs. Lincoln was trying to help him. I saw two men struggling, and then I saw John Wilkes Booth leap to the stage, shouting, "Sic semper tyrannis!" He caught his boot and fell. He apparently was hurt, because he was limping badly as he ran.

I made my way to the presidential box and tried to comfort Mrs. Lincoln. I stayed with Mrs. Lincoln and Miss Clara Harris, who had attended the performance that evening with her fiancé, Major Rathbone, the president, and Mrs. Lincoln. Miss Harris and I remained with Mrs. Lincoln until after the president passed away the next morning.

I've known John for years. He had a terrible burden with a father and brother as famous as Junius and Edwin Booth. He had acted in several Shakespearean plays himself but never received the reviews from the critics that his father and brother had. When I saw him the afternoon of the play, he was not his usual charming self. He was quite a ladies' man, you know. I asked him if he had been working on any new plays. He smiled in a strange sort of way and said, "I am living the greatest role of my life right now. It will go down in history as the finest performance of any of the Booths."

John and I had occasion to have dinner together several months ago. He was very courtly and proud. Throughout dinner, he talked about Mr. Lincoln. John had never met him personally, but he said he hated him for what he was doing to the South. He said the South was a land of fine, proud people, and the North was filled with mercenaries who hoped to use their brute strength to bring the South to its knees. Each time we met after that, his conversation quickly turned to Mr. Lincoln and how evil he was. He felt sure that the people would see this and turn him out of office even though he had just been reelected. He said to me, "He is growing more evil and corrupt every day. Something must be done to stop him!"

From the time I met John as a young boy until that fateful April day, I saw him change from a sweet, generous young lad to a bitter man who was obsessed with a hatred that consumed him.

_____
                                                                                    Affiant

SWORN TO AND SUBSCRIBED before me this _____ day of _____ ,

in the year _____ .

_____
NOTARY PUBLIC
State of _____
My Commission Expires:

Formulating Questions for Direct Examination and Cross-Examination

You may wish to use the following questions as guidelines to help the students prepare for direct examination and cross-examination. See the instructions on page 54 in the mock trial *The State v. Hansel Schmidt and Gretel Schmidt* for more detailed information.

The following example shows possible approaches by the prosecution and the defense to the same question.

> *Example:* Why did Detective John F. Parker accept the assignment to protect the president?

> *Prosecution:* It was a great honor to be chosen to protect the president of the United States.

> *Defense:* He viewed it as an easy assignment that allowed him to be excused from duty in the Army.

1. Why would Mary Surratt and George Atzerodt be willing witnesses for the prosecution?

2. Might there be reasons, other than those stated in his affidavit, why Detective John Parker left his post outside the presidential box?

3. How objective can Edwin Booth be as a defense witness?

4. Why would John Wilkes Booth change his plan from abducting the president to assassinating him and the vice president and secretary of state?

5. What was the significance of John Wilkes Booth's actions immediately before the assassination?

6. Did Dr. Samuel Mudd really fail to recognize John Wilkes Booth when he treated his injured leg?

CAUTION: Remind the students that an attorney never asks a question on cross-examination unless he or she knows the answer the witness will give.

IN THE UNITED STATES
DISTRICT COURT
FOR THE DISTRICT OF COLUMBIA

THE UNITED STATES OF AMERICA,
  Plaintiff,

-v-

CASE NO.: 65-13-CF

JOHN WILKES BOOTH,
  Defendant

JURY BALLOT

_V E R D I C T_

Please circle your choice:

To the charge of first degree murder, John Wilkes Booth is

    GUILTY   NOT GUILTY by reason of insanity

To the charge of treason, John Wilkes Booth is

    GUILTY   NOT GUILTY by reason of insanity

SO SAY WE ALL:

DATED in Washington, District of Columbia, this _____ day of _____ ,
in the year _____ .

_____
Foreperson

Bibliography

The following sources were used in preparing this mock trial. Direct quotations found in this mock trial appear in standard accounts of the times.

Bishop, Jim. *The Day Lincoln Was Shot*. New York: Harper & Brothers, 1955.

Campbell, Helen Jones. *Confederate Courier*. New York: St. Martin's Press, 1964.

Jakoubek, Robert E. *The Assassination of Abraham Lincoln*. Brookfield, CT: Millbrook Press, 1993.

O'Neal, Michael. *The Assassination of Abraham Lincoln, Opposing Viewpoints*. San Diego, CA: Greenhaven Press, 1991.

Smith, Gene. *American Gothic: The Story of America's Legendary Theatrical Family—Junius, Edwin and John Wilkes Booth*. New York: Simon & Schuster, 1992.

Weichmann, Louis J. *A True History of the Assassination of Abraham Lincoln and the Conspiracy of 1865*. New York: Vintage Books, 1977.

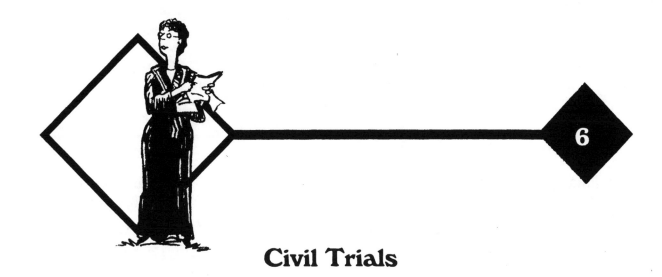

Civil Trials

Overview

Civil cases do not involve violations of laws made by governing bodies. They deal with private problems between individuals or corporations concerning such matters as responsibility for an accident, failure to fulfill the terms of a contract, malpractice, or damages from libel. The public is usually not involved, and each party in the suit engages an attorney to present evidence and question witnesses.

The object of a civil action in which the defendant is judged to be wrong is an attempt to restore the situation to what it would have been had no legal wrong been committed. In most instances, the defendant is ordered to pay the wronged party a sum of money. Other types of ruling include an **injunction** ordering the defendant not to do something or a **judgment** restoring property to its rightful owner.

If the offense is especially serious, the plaintiff may ask for **punitive damages** to punish the defendant. The court may award these if it wishes to impress on the public at large that such offenses will not be tolerated.

In civil cases, a decision is made by a judge or a jury. If a jury hears the case, the verdict need not be unanimo states, four or five out of six jurors will determine the outcome. Check your local courts to find out what procedure they follow.

When considering the evidence, the jury must decide in whose favor the facts weigh most heavily. Unlike criminal trials, in civil trials the jury need not render a verdict based on the absence of a reasonable doubt. A **preponderance of the evidence** decides the verdict.

The civil trials presented in this chapter feature characters easily recognized by your students. The familiar facts have been enhanced to provide the material necessary for a mock trial. The three civil trials that are presented in this book are:

- Jack King and Jill Hamilton v. Harvey Miller - In this adaptation of the nursery rhyme "Jack and Jill" they are suing the owner of the well for not providing adequate protection around the well.
- Dale Hampshire v. Clara Muffet - An adaptation of the nursery rhyme "Little Miss Muffet," this case involves a broken lease agreement due to an infestation of insects.
- Lord Capulet v. Friar Laurence - A retelling of the story of *Romeo and Juliet*, this case alleges that Friar Laurence is guilty of administering an illegal drug and interfering with a marriage contract.

Jack King and Jill Hamilton
v.
Harvey Miller

Background Information

The well-known characters of Jack and Jill have been modernized to suit our needs. Jack King and Jill Hamilton are two teenage neighbors. Jack is experiencing the thrill of being a new driver. As an excuse to drive his car, he offers to take his neighbor, Jill Hamilton, home from her job at the ShopWell supermarket. It's a warm July evening, and rather than go to the neighborhood fast food restaurant for a cold drink, they decide to visit Harvey Miller's well. They rationalize that Mr. Miller lets everyone drink from his well, so they are not **trespassing**.

Jack drives up the hill to the well and parks the car, leaving the headlights on to illuminate the well. He gets a bucket from his trunk and walks over to the well. The area around the well is wet, and Jack slips and falls, breaking the crown on his front tooth. Jill hears the noise of Jack falling with the bucket and gets out of the car to help him. At the same time, Harvey Miller hears the commotion and opens his door to investigate. His dog, Rex, starts barking and runs out of the house. The dog startles Jill, and she tumbles and breaks an arm and a leg.

Jack King and Jill Hamilton believe that Harvey Miller should have had safeguards by his well to protect children from danger. By not doing so, he created an **attractive nuisance**. Jack and Jill are legally minors, so they decide to sue Harvey Miller for damages based on this ordinance.

Harvey Miller says that Jack and Jill were trespassing and that he had attempted to put up "No Trespassing" signs, but they were always stolen. The property has been in his family for generations. Harvey is widowed and retired now and cannot afford to do more than put up the signs.

The plaintiffs' witness, Robin Nelson, and the witness for the defense, Lee Simpson and Jamie Gilbert, have names that are gender neutral; therefore, these individuals may be either male or female.

Definitions

Age of maturity - The age at which an individual shall be considered an adult; age 18.

Assumption of risk - The deliberate choice of an individual to risk a known danger.

Attractive nuisance - Something that is dangerous to children; attractive, alluring, or enticing to them; and allows children themselves to create danger out of it. Persons with such an object or condition on their premises owe a duty to protect children from such danger.

Contributory negligence - Occurs when an individual's conduct falls below the standard to which he or she is required to conform for his or her protection; the standard is that of a reasonable person under the circumstances.

Punitive damages - Damages awarded by the court to punish a defendant, as for a serious wrong.

Trespass - An unlawful intentional intrusion on another person's property or person.

Exhibits

- The pail Jack Hamilton used to get the water
- Muddied shoes or clothes that Jill was wearing
- Diagram showing the location of the house in relation to the well and street (optional)

Trial Participants

Plaintiff	*Defense*
Attorney(s)	Attorney(s)
Jack King, Plaintiff	Harvey Miller, Defendant
Jill Hamilton, Plaintiff	Jamie Gilbert
Robin Nelson	Lee Simpson

> **Pages 104 - 117 can be reproduced and used as beginning documents to present this mock trial.**

IN THE CIRCUIT COURT OF THE
FOURTH JUDICIAL CIRCUIT, IN AND
FOR COLLIER COUNTY, _____

JACK KING and
JILL HAMILTON,
  Plaintiffs,
-v-
HARVEY MILLER,
  Defendant

CASE NO.: 97-041-CA

STATEMENT OF FACTS

At 9:10 p.m. on July 15, plaintiff, Jack King, age 17, drove his car up a hill commonly known to residents of Ferndale as Miller's Hill. Plaintiff, Jill Hamilton, age 16, was a passenger. When the car reached the top of the hill, Jack King stopped the car and shut off its engine but left the headlights on. He got out of the car, opened the trunk of the car, and took out a pail. He then walked over to a well, which was on the property of defendant, Harvey Miller. The headlights of the car lit Jack King's path. He lowered the bucket into the well, filled it, and lifted it back out of the well. As he turned to take the bucket back to the car, he tripped and fell, breaking the crown on his tooth. Upon seeing him fall, Jill Hamilton got out of the car and ran to his rescue. At that moment, a large Doberman dog came running from the Miller residence. He barked loudly, startling Ms. Hamilton. She ran back to the car, slipped on a wet spot on the ground, and came tumbling after Jack King. As a result of the fall, she broke her left leg and right arm.

The plaintiffs have filed suit against Harvey Miller, alleging that the well was an attractive nuisance; that Jack King's fall was caused by tripping over a loose rock from the side of the well; that Jill Hamilton's injury was caused by poor conditions around the well, which caused a slippery situation; and that Mr. Miller's Doberman had not been kept on a leash. They are asking for a settlement of $500 to cover dental bills for Jack King and $3,000 to cover medical bills for Jill Hamilton. Ms. Hamilton is also asking for $2,000 in lost wages because she was unable to perform her duties as a checker at ShopWell. Ms. Hamilton is also asking for $10,000 for pain and suffering caused by the injuries.

The defendant denies any liability for injuries and suffering. He claims that Jack King and Jill Hamilton are guilty of contributory negligence not only by trespassing on his property, but also by doing so at night when visibility was limited.

The amounts for medical bills and wages are stipulated and need not be proven at trial. Any amount for pain and suffering is at issue.

IN THE CIRCUIT COURT OF THE
FOURTH JUDICIAL CIRCUIT, IN AND
FOR COLLIER COUNTY, _____

JACK KING and
JILL HAMILTON,
  Plaintiffs,

-v-

HARVEY MILLER,
  Defendant

CASE NO.: 97-041-CA

GENERAL AFFIDAVIT

_____*Jack King*_____ , being first duly sworn according to law, deposes and says that:
     Affiant

    My name is Jack King, and I live at 838 Cherry Lane in Ferndale. I have lived here all of my life. On the evening of July 15, I picked up my neighbor, Jill Hamilton, from work at the ShopWell supermarket. Because it was such a warm evening, we decided to go for a ride to Old Man Miller's place to get some water from his well. His real name is Harvey Miller, but everyone calls him Old Man Miller. The water from his well is famous around the town. It tastes very good, not like the water you get from the faucet. The street next to his property is called Miller's Lane. I guess it gets its name from him.

    Well, anyway, I drove up the hill, parked the car, and shut off the engine. My dad always told me to shut the engine off if I was not in the car, just to be safe. I did leave the headlights on so I could see where I was walking. I got a clean bucket with a lid on it out of the trunk of the car. We use the bucket for drinking water on the job when I cut lawns during the summer. I lowered the bucket into the well, filled it, and lifted it out. As I turned to take the bucket back to the car, I tripped over a rock and fell and broke the crown on my front tooth. Jill heard the commotion and got out of the car. She ran to help me. Just then, I heard this dog barking. The sound seemed to come closer and closer. Jill screamed and tried to get back to the car. She must have slipped on some mud that was around the well. She tumbled down the hill to where I was. She started crying, and I could see she was in terrible pain.

General Affidavit continues on page 106.

At that time, Old Man Miller showed up. He said something about kids trespassing all the time. When he saw Jill, he ran back to the house and called the police. He returned, and in a little while, the police and an ambulance showed up. They took Jill to the hospital.

I went to the dentist, and he said that the crown on my tooth could not be fixed. I had to have a new false tooth put in. It cost $500.

_____
Affiant

SWORN TO AND SUBSCRIBED before me this _____ day of _____ , in the year _____.

_____

NOTARY PUBLIC
State of _____
My Commission Expires:

IN THE CIRCUIT COURT OF THE
FOURTH JUDICIAL CIRCUIT, IN AND
FOR COLLIER COUNTY, _____

JACK KING and
JILL HAMILTON,
   Plaintiffs,
-v-

CASE NO.: 97-041-CA

HARVEY MILLER,
   Defendant

GENERAL AFFIDAVIT

_____*Jill Hamilton*_____, being first duly sworn according to law, deposes and says that:
      Affiant

    My name is Jill Hamilton, and I live at 834 Cherry Lane in Ferndale. I have lived there since I was in the seventh grade.

    On the evening of July 15, I worked the evening shift at ShopWell. Jack King, who is my neighbor, had just gotten his driver's license. He stopped by the supermarket and asked if I wanted to go for a ride. This was about 8:30 p.m. I told him I did, and when I got off at 8:45 p.m., we got into his car. He suggested that we go for a soda at Burger Heaven. I said I didn't feel like having anything sweet. He then said he had a great idea. There was a well on Mr. Miller's place that had the best water. It was always icy cold and didn't taste like the water we get from the faucet. He said the kids went there all the time to get water.

    We drove up the hill. Jack parked the car and turned off the engine but left the headlights on so he could see his way to the well. I sat in the car because I didn't know the area. I watched as he drew the water from the well. Suddenly, I heard this crash, and then Jack was groaning and holding his face. I jumped out of the car to help him. As I went to help him, I heard a terrific commotion and a dog barking and growling. When I looked up, I saw a big black dog running toward me. I screamed and tried to get back to the car.

General Affidavit continues on page 108.

As I did so, I had to go near the well. There was no grass there, and the ground was wet and slippery. I lost my footing and went tumbling down the hill to where Jack was. I was in terrible pain, and I guess I started crying. Mr. Miller came out, said something, and left. I guess he called the police because he came back, and in a short while a police car and then an ambulance came.

They took me to the hospital. The X-rays showed I had a broken right arm and broken left leg. My medical bills were $3,000. Because I couldn't go to work, I also lost more than $2,000 in wages from my job at ShopWell. I couldn't go to summer school for a month, and my arm and leg still hurt when the weather is damp.

_____
Affiant

SWORN TO AND SUBSCRIBED before me this _____ day of _____ ,

in the year _____.

_____
NOTARY PUBLIC
State of _____
My Commission Expires:

IN THE CIRCUIT COURT OF THE
FOURTH JUDICIAL CIRCUIT, IN AND
FOR COLLIER COUNTY, _____

JACK KING and
JILL HAMILTON,
  Plaintiffs,
-v-
HARVEY MILLER,
  Defendant

CASE NO.: 97-041-CA

════════════════════════════════════

GENERAL AFFIDAVIT

════════════════════════════════════

_____Robin Nelson_____, being first duly sworn according to law, deposes and says that:
     Affiant

    My name is Robin Nelson. I live at 43 Parker Lane, Cedar Hills. I've lived there all my life. I'm 19 years old. Even though Cedar Hills is a neighboring town, everyone there knows about Old Man Miller's—I mean Mr. Miller's—well. The water is so clear and tastes better than any water you get out of a bottle or the faucet. We've gone there many times to get water. Sometimes we ask Mr. Miller, and sometimes, if he's not around, we just take the water. He never says no, so we're sure he wouldn't mind.

    One thing that always worried me was that anyone could get water from that well. He didn't have it fenced in or anything. I also was afraid that some little kid might come by and fall in and drown. When you lowered a pail in, it took an awful long time before you heard it hit the water, so the well must have been awfully deep.

    I work with Jill and saw her at the hospital the day after the accident. She was in bad shape. She's come back to work, but she's not as fast checking as she once was.

_____
                                 Affiant

SWORN TO AND SUBSCRIBED before me this _____ day of _____,
in the year _____.

_____
NOTARY PUBLIC
State of _____
My Commission Expires:

IN THE CIRCUIT COURT OF THE
FOURTH JUDICIAL CIRCUIT, IN AND
FOR COLLIER COUNTY, _____

JACK KING and
JILL HAMILTON,
 Plaintiffs,
-v-

CASE NO.: 97-041-CA

HARVEY MILLER,
 Defendant

GENERAL AFFIDAVIT

_____*Harvey Miller*_____, being first duly sworn according to law, deposes and says that:
          Affiant

My name is Harvey Miller, and I live at 1 Miller's Lane. I've lived in my house all my life, and so did my father and his father before him. I used to own about 20 acres and farmed it, but about 25 years ago, I realized it was just too much land for me. I sold part of it to a developer, and he built a group of houses down the hill. They named the road that leads up to my house "Miller's Lane" because the land had belonged to Millers for more than 100 years.

I remember when my father and grandfather dug the well at the top of the hill. I was a little boy. The water from that well was the best around. It's the only water I use for drinking or making coffee or tea. It used to be that I'd let anyone take water from the well, but then too many people started coming. I put up a "No Trespassing" sign to discourage people from just taking water. Still, if any of the kids asked me or someone came to the door, I never said no. I thought I was just being a good neighbor.

On July 15, at about a little after 9 p.m., I heard a car come up the hill. I don't get many visitors, so when a car comes up the road, both Rex and I take notice. Then I didn't hear anything, so I thought I was mistaken. A few minutes later, I heard a sound. It sounded as if something had fallen. I opened the door to look outside, and Rex ran out. Rex usually is not a barker, but I guess he was scared and started barking and running toward the noise. He did that once when a skunk knocked over my garbage can. That time, I had to use about two gallons of tomato juice to get the smell out of Rex.

Anyway, when I looked out, I saw a car parked on the road with its headlights shining on the well. I realized right then that some fool kid had come up to get water. I heard a scream and then someone crying. When I walked over to the car, I saw this girl on the ground, obviously in pain. There was a young fella with her. I had seen him before, but I didn't know his name. I ran back to the house and called the police and told them that someone was hurt and we'd probably need an ambulance. They got there within a few minutes.

I really don't understand this lawsuit. Here I am being a good neighbor and letting the kids get water from the well. I've never said no if they asked for it, but I did object to them just taking it. I think everyone knew how I felt. Now we have someone who not only took the water without asking but did it at night. These fool kids do something stupid and then they expect me to pay for their stupidity.

_____
Affiant

SWORN TO AND SUBSCRIBED before me this _____ day of _____ ,
in the year _____ .

_____
NOTARY PUBLIC
State of _____
My Commission Expires:

IN THE CIRCUIT COURT OF THE
FOURTH JUDICIAL CIRCUIT, IN AND
FOR COLLIER COUNTY, _____

JACK KING and
JILL HAMILTON,
  Plaintiffs,
-v-

CASE NO.: 97-041-CA

HARVEY MILLER,
  Defendant

GENERAL AFFIDAVIT

_____ *Jamie Gilbert* _____ , being first duly sworn according to law, deposes and says that:
Affiant

My name is Jamie Gilbert. I live at 10 Miller's Lane, Ferndale. When Harvey Miller subdivided his farm 25 years ago, I was one of the first to buy one of the new homes that were built. I grew up in Ferndale, and I remember when I was little, if we saw Mr. Miller or his wife outside, they'd always invite us to have a drink of cool well water.

Mr. Miller's wife died about eight years ago, and he lives there alone with Rex, his big black Doberman. Rex looks fierce, but he is really scared of his own shadow. Mr. Miller is retired and really doesn't get around too well. I don't think he has too much money. He's had the same old plaid winter coat for as long as I can remember.

On the night of July 15, I was sitting in my backyard watching the fireflies. I heard a car go by. I thought it unusual as any car going past our house is either coming from or going to Mr. Miller's house. I figured maybe an old friend had come to visit. A little while later, I heard Rex barking. Rex is not a barker, so I was afraid that some harm had come to Mr. Miller. When I looked out, I saw the car by the well with its headlights on and Mr. Miller going back to his house as fast as he could. He seemed to be all right, so I didn't think any more of it. In a few minutes, a police car and then an ambulance came. Everyone in the neighborhood came out, and we saw them putting this young girl in the ambulance.

It was only later that we found out what had happened. Can you imagine! Someone is trespassing at night and stealing water from a well, and then they have the nerve to sue poor Mr. Miller. He had put up several "No Trespassing" signs, but the kids always stole them as souvenirs. What's he supposed to do? Take down his well or put a big fence around it? He doesn't have the money for that. It's a shame a person can't enjoy his own property without having to worry about being sued—and, worse still, sued by a trespasser.

_____

Affiant

SWORN TO AND SUBSCRIBED before me this _____ day of _____ ,
in the year _____ .

_____

NOTARY PUBLIC
State of _____
My Commission Expires:

IN THE CIRCUIT COURT OF THE
FOURTH JUDICIAL CIRCUIT, IN AND
FOR COLLIER COUNTY, _____

JACK KING and
JILL HAMILTON,
  Plaintiffs,
-v-

CASE NO.: 97-041-CA

HARVEY MILLER,
  Defendant

GENERAL AFFIDAVIT

_____*Lee Simpson*_____ , being first duly sworn according to law, deposes and says that:
Affiant

My name is Lee Simpson. I am a police officer for the Ferndale Police Department. On the evening of July 15, at 9:25 p.m., I received a call from headquarters to investigate an accident at the residence of Harvey Miller. An ambulance had also been summoned as a young female was reported to have been injured.

When I arrived on the scene, I observed a blue Toyota, license plate Z5-98T, parked with its headlights on. The engine was not running. Lying on the grass about 25 feet down the hill and to the left of the driver's side of the vehicle was a young female, later identified as Jill Hamilton, age 16. She complained of pain in her right forearm and left ankle. Her companion, Jack King, age 17, was kneeling by her side trying to assist her.

When questioned, Jack King said that they had parked the car on the road and gone over to the well, which was on Harvey Miller's property, to get water. As he was carrying the water back to the car, he tripped over a large rock, which investigation later proved to be a part of the top of the rim of the well. The mortar holding the rock had apparently worn away, allowing the rock to come loose. Around the well, the ground was muddy because there was no grass. Jill Hamilton was injured trying to aid her companion, Jack King. She claims to have been frightened by Mr. Miller's Doberman, which had barked loudly. The dog came to within a distance of about 20 feet but did not touch her.

The ambulance came and took Miss Hamilton to the hospital, and her parents were notified. Jack King's father was called to take his son home. When his father came, he commented that the crown on his son's front tooth had been badly damaged.

I've known Mr. Miller for years. He's well known around these parts. When I talked with him in the past, he had complained about people taking his water without asking. He had put up "No Trespassing" signs on several occasions, but they always seemed to disappear.

_____

Affiant

SWORN TO AND SUBSCRIBED before me this _____ day of _____ , in the year _____ .

_____

NOTARY PUBLIC
State of _____
My Commission Expires:

Formulating Questions for Direct Examination and Cross-Examination

The cases presented in the mock trials in this book are purposely ambiguous. There are no clear-cut solutions. It is up to the attorneys to explore the affidavits for factual weaknesses and inconsistencies. It is important that the attorneys regard all affidavits in this way, not just those of the opposition, so that they can prepare for cross-examination. The student attorneys should be especially careful to analyze the affidavits to determine which information is factual and which is opinion. *Opinions are only admissible as testimony if offered by an expert witness.* An example would be an orthopedic surgeon's opinion as to whether a leg injury might impair an individual's ability to perform necessary duties at work.

I have found it best to allow the students to explore their own ideas first. Then ask them specific questions and have them suggest possible ways that both the plaintiff and defense attorneys might approach each issue. By doing this, the students come to understand that they must look at all aspects of the case from both sides.

Example: Were Jack King and Jill Hamilton guilty of stealing Harvey Miller's water?

Plaintiff: No. Mr. Miller had allowed others to take water from the well in the past and made no effort to bring charges against them.

Defense: Yes. The well was on Mr. Miller's property, and by taking the water, the plaintiffs were guilty of stealing.

The following are examples of questions that might be used to help students explore the issues in the civil trial, *Jack King and Jill Hamilton v. Harvey Miller*:

1. Is the time of day at which the accident occurred significant in this case?

2. Why didn't Harvey Miller realize that the well could pose a danger to children?

3. When they trespassed on Mr. Miller's property at night, didn't Jack King and Jill Hamilton assume certain risks?

4. Weren't the neighbors aware that Harvey Miller's unprotected well might be a danger to children?

5. Because the police were aware of the well's existence, couldn't they have done something to make sure that no one was injured?

6. If Robin Nelson was so worried about a child falling into the well, why wasn't some action taken?

7. How should the "age of maturity" be applied in this case?

8. Are Mr. Miller's age and financial situation factors to consider in reaching a decision in this trial?

9. Does Mr. Miller have an obligation to control his dog better?

10. Why did Jack King turn off his car's engine when he stopped to get water from the well?

11. As owner of the well, what obligation does Harvey Miller have to others who might be endangered by his well?

CAUTION: Remind the students that an attorney never asks a question on cross-examination unless he or she knows the answer the witness will give.

IN THE CIRCUIT COURT OF THE
FOURTH JUDICIAL CIRCUIT, IN AND
FOR COLLIER COUNTY, _____

JACK KING and
JILL HAMILTON,
  Plaintiffs,
-v-
HARVEY MILLER,
  Defendant

CASE NO.: 97-041-CA

═══

JURY BALLOT

═══

V E R D I C T

Please circle your choice:

      YES   Harvey Miller shall be held responsible for the accident involving Jack King and Jill Hamilton and should pay $500 for Jack King's dental bills and $3,000 for Jill Hamilton's medical bills.

OR

      NO   Harvey Miller shall not be held responsible for the accident involving Jack King and Jill Hamilton.

* *

If you voted NO, *stop here*. DO NOT CONTINUE.
If you voted YES, *continue*.

Harvey Miller should have to pay for Jill Hamilton's lost wages in the amount of $2,000.

    Circle one: YES   NO

Harvey Miller should have to pay for Jill Hamilton's pain and suffering.

    Circle one: YES   NO

If you voted YES, list the amount between $1 and $10,000 to be awarded to Jill Hamilton for pain and suffering.

Amount for pain and suffering $ _____

DATED in Fernville, Collier County, _____ , this _____ day of _____ , in the year _____ .

_____
Foreperson

Dale Hampshire
v.
Clara Muffet

Background Information

In this updated version of the popular nursery rhyme, Miss Muffet is a modern-day woman. She is well educated and is striving to become independent. Her first step is to move into her own apartment. She has been living with her parents, but after working for several years as a dental assistant, she believes she can now afford to be on her own.

She finds the apartment of her dreams in the Arachnid Arms. The landlord, Dale Hampshire, agrees to rent the apartment to her for $700 a month. She signs a one-year **lease**, that takes effect February 1 and gives one month's rent as a security deposit. She is responsible for paying the electric bill.

Early in April, according to Miss Muffet, she claims she saw a black widow spider. She reported it to Dale Hampshire, who called Bugs-No-Moore, the exterminator who usually services the apartments. Miss Muffet claims she continued to see spiders after Bugs-No-Moore treated the apartment and reported this to the landlord. In mid-July, as she was sitting in her beanbag chair eating yogurt, a large spider crawled across her leg. Feeling she could not stay in the apartment that night, she left and the following day moved her belongings to her parents' home. She stopped paying rent on the apartment.

Dale Hampshire has brought suit, charging that she has violated the terms of her lease and owes rent for the remainder of the contract.

Clara Muffet counters that Dale Hampshire had an obligation as landlord to keep her apartment in a livable condition and that this was not done.

The principals in this trial, with the exception of Clara Muffet, have names that are gender neutral and could be either male or female.

Definitions

Lease - A contract by which one conveys real estate for a specified term and for a specific rent.

Security - Something given, deposited, or pledged to make certain the fulfillment of an obligation.

Exhibits

- Rental agreement between Dale Hampshire and Clara Muffet
- Invoice from Bugs-No-Moore for treatment of Clara Muffet's apartment
  (portions of this invoice have been left blank to be completed by the teacher or students involved in the plaintiff's legal action. It is especially interesting to note how observant students are of the type of insecticide used. This can be an issue and can call for some research.)
- Site plan of the apartment (optional)

Trial Participants

Plaintiff	*Defense*
Attorney(s)	Attorney(s)
Dale Hampshire, Plaintiff	Clara Muffet, Defendant
Robin Moore	Jean Lewis
Kit Smith	Dr. Lee McGuiness
Gale Johnston	

> **Pages 120 - 135 can be reproduced and used as beginning documents to present this mock trial.**

Rental Agreement Between Dale Hampshire and Clara Muffet

Rental Agreement

THIS AGREEMENT, Made and executed this _1st_ day of _February_, A.D. _____, by and between _Dale Hampshire_, hereinafter called the Landlord, and _Clara Muffet_, hereinafter called the Tenant.

WITNESSETH, THAT Landlord does hereby let unto Tenant the premises known as Apartment _3-A_ at _Arachnid Arms Apartments_ for the term commencing the _1st_ day of _February_, _____ and fully ending at midnight on the last day of _January_, _____, at and for the total rent of _8400.00_ dollars, the first installment payable on the signing of this agreement and the remaining installments payable in advance on the _1st_ day of each ensuing month, to and at the office of _Dale Hampshire at the Arachnid Arms Apartments_.

On the _1st day_ of _February_, _____ a sum of _$700_ shall become due and payable. This sum shall cover the period up to the last day of _February_, _____; thereafter, a sum of _$700.00_ shall be due and payable on the _1st_ day of each month.

AND TENANT does hereby agree as follows:

1. Tenant will pay the rent at the time specified.
2. Tenant will pay all utility bills as they become due.
3. Tenant will use the premises for a dwelling and for no other purpose.
4. Tenant will not use said premises for any unlawful purpose, or in any noisy or rowdy manner or in a way offensive to any other occupant of the building.
5. Landlord shall have access to the premises at any time for the purposes of inspection, to make repairs the Landlord considers necessary, or to show the apartment to tenant applicants.
6. Tenant will give Landlord prompt notice of any defects or breakage in the structure, equipment, or fixtures of said premises.
7. Tenant will pay a security deposit in the amount of _$700.00_, which will be held by Landlord until expiration of this lease and refunded on the condition that said premises is returned in good condition, normal wear and tear excepted.
8. Tenant will not keep pets, live animals, or birds of any description on said premises.
9. Landlord shall not be liable for damage to property of Tenant caused by rodents, rain, snow, defective plumbing, or any other source.
10. Tenant shall be required to give the Landlord at least thirty (30) days notice, in writing, of his or her intention to vacate the premises at the expiration of this tenancy. If Tenant vacates the premises without first furnishing said notice, Tenant will be liable to the Landlord for one month's rent.
11. Tenant agrees to observe all such rules and regulations which the Landlord or his agents will make concerning the apartment building.

IN TESTIMONY WHEREOF, Landlord and Tenant have signed this agreement.

signed in the presence of: Date _____

_____

Elvira Klutz   _____
Notary   Dale Hampshire
(Commission expires _____)

_____
Clara Muffet

Blank Bugs-No-Moore Invoice

Bugs-No-Moore

Keeping Homes Bug-Free Since 1985

Robin Moore, Certified Exterminator
State License 6958

Service Slip/Invoice

Bill to:

Dale Hampshire
Arachnid Arms Apartments

Site Serviced: ___Apt. 3-A___   **Date Serviced:** ___April 10,___

Description of Service: _____

_____

Pesticide Used: _____

_____

Technician: _____

Comments: _____

_____

_____

_____

**A Bug-Free Home
is a Happy Home**

IN THE COUNTY COURT OF THE
THIRD JUDICIAL CIRCUIT, IN AND
FOR WEBSTER COUNTY, _____

DALE HAMPSHIRE,
  Plaintiff,
-v-

CASE NO.: 98-88-CA

CLARA MUFFET,
  Defendant

STATEMENT OF FACTS

On February 1, Clara Muffet signed a lease with Dale Hampshire to rent Apartment 3-A in the Arachnid Arms Apartments. The term of the lease was for one year at $700 per month with an option to renew. Ms. Muffet paid a $700 security deposit and was to pay the monthly electric bill. She moved into the apartment on February 1. Early in April, Ms. Muffet reported to Dale Hampshire that she had seen a black widow spider. The owner called Bugs-No-Moore, a local exterminator, who treated the apartment for spider infestation.

Ms. Muffet continued to report seeing spiders and other insects. On July 14, she reported that a large spider startled her as she was sitting on her beanbag chair, eating yogurt. She left the premises immediately and spent the night at her parents' home.

The next day, she moved out of the apartment. Dale Hampshire alleges that she violated her lease because she refuses to pay her rent. The defendant states that she should not have to pay her rent because the apartment is not a fit place in which to live. She has asked the plaintiff to use her $700 security deposit for the August rent. The plaintiff says she still owes the rent for September, October, November, December, and January.

IN THE COUNTY COURT OF THE
THIRD JUDICIAL CIRCUIT, IN AND
FOR WEBSTER COUNTY, _____

DALE HAMPSHIRE,
   Plaintiff,

-v-

CLARA MUFFET,
   Defendant

CASE NO.: 98-88-CA

GENERAL AFFIDAVIT

_____*Dale Hampshire*_____ , being first duly sworn according to law, deposes and says that:
        Affiant

    I am the owner and manager of the Arachnid Arms Apartments. I have lived there for 13 years since the apartments were built. There are 15 units, all of them on the ground level. Part of the attraction of these apartments is their beautiful location. I made sure when they were built that as few trees as possible were cut down.

    Most of the tenants have lived there for many years, and they all seem to be very satisfied.

    I rented apartment 3-A to Clara Muffet on February 1, ____. She signed a one-year renewable lease specifying a rental rate of $700 a month, plus a $700 security deposit. I hesitated to rent it to her. I always require references to make sure that we get the right kind of tenants. You can't be too careful. Anyway, she had a letter from her boss, a dentist who said she was very trustworthy. I knew that she had always lived with her parents and that this was her first time on her own.

    Early in April, she complained about a black widow spider. I can assure you that none of my other tenants nor I have ever seen one. I'm sure they would have been quick to tell me about it if they had. I called Bugs-No-Moore, and they treated the area outside of her apartment. I've dealt with Bugs-No-Moore for years and know the business to be reputable.

General Affidavit continues on page 124.

Bugs-No-Moore owner Robin Moore said the treatment was done by the service person as effectively as possible; however, Ms. Muffet had so many plants on her patio that he was afraid to spray too close to them and possibly kill them. The service person also said that the plants might be attracting the spiders. People want to have all of these plants around but don't realize the problems they can cause.

At any rate, I came home on the afternoon of July 15 and saw a rental truck in front of Ms. Muffet's apartment. When I asked her about it, she said the place wasn't fit to live in. I told her she had signed a contract and had to pay me rent through the rest of the year. I had fulfilled my part of the contract and kept her apartment in good repair and in livable condition. She had to fulfill hers. She said I should use the $700 security deposit for August's rent and then find someone else to pay the rent for September through January.

It's not that easy to rent an apartment these days. By the time I advertise and get someone in here, six months could pass. Ms. Muffet signed a contract, and she must live up to it.

_____

                                                              Affiant

SWORN TO AND SUBSCRIBED before me this _____ day of _____ ,

in the year _____ .

_____

NOTARY PUBLIC
State of _____
My Commission Expires:

IN THE COUNTY COURT OF THE
THIRD JUDICIAL CIRCUIT, IN AND
FOR WEBSTER COUNTY, _____

DALE HAMPSHIRE,
  Plaintiff,
-v-
CLARA MUFFET,
  Defendant

CASE NO.: 98-88-CA

GENERAL AFFIDAVIT

_____*Robin Moore*_____ , being first duly sworn according to law, deposes and says that:
      Affiant

    My name is Robin Moore, and I am the owner of Bugs-No-Moore, one of the largest exterminating companies in the area. Our company has serviced Dale Hampshire's Arachnid Arms Apartments ever since they were built 13 years ago.

    We regularly treat for termites and occasionally for ant infestation. When Dale Hampshire called me in early April about a possible black widow spider problem, I promptly sent out one of my most experienced people. He said he did not see any spiders, but he did spray the area around Ms. Muffet's apartment. He did report she had many plants there, and he was afraid to move them or spray on them for fear of damaging them.

    I told Dale Hampshire that we had treated the area as best we could and that Ms. Muffet's plants had prevented us from spraying everywhere. You know, people don't realize that having plants outside their home—especially near a wooded area—can draw all kinds of insects.

_____
                    Affiant

SWORN TO AND SUBSCRIBED before me this _____ day of _____ ,
in the year _____.

_____
NOTARY PUBLIC
State of _____
My Commission Expires:

IN THE COUNTY COURT OF THE
THIRD JUDICIAL CIRCUIT, IN AND
FOR WEBSTER COUNTY, _____

DALE HAMPSHIRE,
  Plaintiff,
-v-
CLARA MUFFET,
  Defendant

CASE NO.: 98-88-CA

GENERAL AFFIDAVIT

_____*Kit Smith*_____ , being first duly sworn according to law, deposes and says that:
   Affiant

    I've lived at the Arachnid Arms Apartments for almost seven years. My apartment is right next to the one that Clara Muffet had rented. That apartment must have a revolving door. It seems that every time I turn around, there is a new tenant living there. I cannot understand why. I love living here. It is so pleasant with the woods in the back. Just like living in the country. Occasionally, I see a bug or two—maybe even a spider—but not enough to make me want to move. I'm a member of the Animal Rights League, and I feel that spiders are nature's creatures and deserve to live, too.

    I was really surprised that Clara was so squeamish about spiders. She was always working on her plants on the patio. She had many different varieties—all of them very beautiful. Usually people who like to garden don't let bugs upset them.

    Whatever happened, I think she really overreacted. I had seen one of those spiders she was talking about. They are perfectly harmless. They usually don't stay. They're usually just temporary visitors.

_____
                                    Affiant

SWORN TO AND SUBSCRIBED before me this _____ day of _____ ,
in the year _____.

_____
NOTARY PUBLIC
State of _____
My Commission Expires:

IN THE COUNTY COURT OF THE
THIRD JUDICIAL CIRCUIT, IN AND
FOR WEBSTER COUNTY, _____

DALE HAMPSHIRE,
   Plaintiff,
-v-
CLARA MUFFET,
   Defendant

CASE NO.: 98-88-CA

GENERAL AFFIDAVIT

_____*Gale Johnston*_____ , being first duly sworn according to law, deposes and says that:
        Affiant

    My name is Gale Johnston, and I work in the office next to the one where Clara Muffet works. A group of us who work in the same building often have lunch together.

    I remember when Clara first moved into her new apartment. She was really excited. It was the first time she was on her own. She invited us to see the place, and I must say she had furnished it very nicely and expensively. I used to work for a furniture store, so I know something about the cost of furniture. I asked her how she could afford the rent and furniture. She said it was tight, but she was managing. I wondered about this, especially because she had just bought a late-model Toyota.

    In June she went on vacation to Bermuda. When she came back, she said she had really spent more than she intended because the shops in Bermuda were wonderful. Her comment was that she had "maxed out her credit card." I guess she used up all of her available credit and was going to have to start paying her bills.

    If you ask me, I think she moved out because she was living beyond her means. The "spider story" was her way of getting out of her lease.

_____
          Affiant

SWORN TO AND SUBSCRIBED before me this _____ day of _____ ,
in the year _____.

_____
NOTARY PUBLIC
State of _____
My Commission Expires:

IN THE COUNTY COURT OF THE
THIRD JUDICIAL CIRCUIT, IN AND
FOR WEBSTER COUNTY, _____

DALE HAMPSHIRE,
 Plaintiff,
-v-
CLARA MUFFET,
 Defendant

CASE NO.: 98-88-CA

GENERAL AFFIDAVIT

_____*Clara Muffet*_____ , being first duly sworn according to law, deposes and says that:
Affiant

My name is Clara Muffet, and I live at 13 Shadyside Lane in Elms Grove. I work as a dental assistant at the office of Dr. Lee McGuiness. I've worked there for four years since I graduated from the local community college.

I have lived at my current address since July 15. This is my parents' home and the home where I grew up.

On February 1, I moved into my own apartment at the Arachnid Arms Apartments. It was a lovely four-room apartment in a beautiful location. It was on the ground floor and had a patio that faced out onto a small wooded area. There was room on the side for me to park my new Toyota. I signed a one-year lease for $700 a month rent with the landlord, Dale Hampshire. This lease could be renewed each year. My rent was $700 a month, and I also paid $700 as a security deposit. In addition, I had to pay my electric bill, which amounted to about $60 a month.

All was well until the warm weather came in April. I noticed there were many different kinds of bugs of the creepy crawly variety. My parents' home had trees around it, but I never saw this many bugs there.

One day, as I came in through my patio door, I noticed a black spider with an hour-glass on its back. Recognizing this as a black widow, I notified my landlord, Dale Hampshire, who claimed that I was mistaken because a black widow spider had never been seen in the 13 years since the apartments were built. The landlord did promise to call Bugs-No-Moore, a local exterminator.

Several days later, when I arrived home from work, I found a note on the front door from Robin Moore of Bugs-No-Moore, saying that the grounds around my apartment had been treated for insects. The note did not say what kind of insecticide had been used.

Within a week, the creepy crawly things started to appear in greater numbers. There were millipedes, centipedes, and several varieties of spiders. I had taken a course in biology, so I was familiar with these insects. I called the landlord to say that matters were worse. Dale Hampshire accused me of exaggerating, that no one else was complaining, and that I must be doing something to attract the bugs.

Finally, on the evening of July 14, I was relaxing in my living room watching TV. I have this wonderful beanbag chair, and I was enjoying a cup of yogurt. Suddenly, I felt something brush against my leg. I looked down and saw this huge, black, hairy spider. That was it! I ran out, got in my car, and drove to my parents' house. There was no way I was going to sleep in that apartment and maybe have something crawl over me.

The next day, I called my friend, Jean Lewis, to help me. As we were moving the furniture, one of those horrible spiders crawled out from under the sofa. We got a plastic container and captured it as evidence.

Dale Hampshire says I have broken the lease that I signed and that I owe rent from August through January. I say the apartment was not fit to live in because the landlord did not see that the bugs were kept under control.

_____
Affiant

SWORN TO AND SUBSCRIBED before me this _____ day of _____ ,
in the year _____ .

_____
NOTARY PUBLIC
State of _____
My Commission Expires:

IN THE COUNTY COURT OF THE
THIRD JUDICIAL CIRCUIT, IN AND
FOR WEBSTER COUNTY, _____

DALE HAMPSHIRE,
  Plaintiff,
-v-
CLARA MUFFET,
  Defendant

CASE NO.: 98-88-CA

GENERAL AFFIDAVIT

_____*Jean Lewis*_____ , being first duly sworn according to law, deposes and says that:
       Affiant

     My name is Jean Lewis. I've known Clara Muffet since grammar school. Clara has always been very conscientious about spending money. I remember she had a paper route as soon as she was old enough to have one. She always was working at some job—mowing lawns, baby-sitting. She knew the value of the dollar and saved carefully. In fact, between the money she saved and scholarships she earned, she was able to pay her full tuition for school to become a dental assistant.

     She lived with her parents while she was going to school. Then she stayed there another year until she got a good job. When she left home, she bought a late-model Toyota. She traded in her previous car, so it really didn't cost that much. Her parents were so proud of her that they helped her buy the furniture for her new apartment.

     She went on vacation to Bermuda with her friend Eloise. They had a wonderful time. When she came back, she said she had spent more than she had planned. Knowing Clara, that wouldn't be too much. She really hated parting with money. She said she "maxed out her credit card." Because it was her first credit card, she only had a credit line of $1,000. Even if she did use it all, her monthly payments couldn't be that high.

Early on the morning of July 15, Clara called me. She was very upset. She told me that she couldn't stay in her apartment any longer because of the spider problem. She asked me if I would help her move. We borrowed a truck from my cousin. When we were moving her furniture, one of those spiders crawled out. We got a plastic container from the kitchen and captured it. I remembered from biology class how to preserve a specimen, so we would have it as proof.

I can't see Clara trying to run out on any agreement. She has too much character to try to cheat anyone.

_____
Affiant

SWORN TO AND SUBSCRIBED before me this _____ day of _____ ,
in the year _____ .

_____
NOTARY PUBLIC
State of _____
My Commission Expires:

IN THE COUNTY COURT OF THE THIRD JUDICIAL CIRCUIT, IN AND FOR WEBSTER COUNTY, _____

DALE HAMPSHIRE,
  Plaintiff,
-v-
CLARA MUFFET,
  Defendant

CASE NO.: 98-88-CA

GENERAL AFFIDAVIT

_____*Dr. Lee McGuiness*_____ , being first duly sworn according to law, deposes and says that:
      Affiant

Clara Muffet has worked for me for a year and a half, and I can vouch that she is honest and hardworking. I certainly would not have given her a letter of recommendation so that she could rent an apartment at Arachnid Arms if I did not believe that she was trustworthy.

Since working for me, I must say that my office has never been neater or cleaner. Clara has a place for everything, and everything is in its place. Some of my other employees complain that she is too particular. They say they can understand the instruments and materials we use in the dental work being scrupulously clean, but they feel she is too particular about the waiting room. They call her the waxing lady because she is always polishing the furniture. I feel it makes our patients comfortable knowing the place is clean everywhere.

She had told me about her problems with the spiders and other insects. At first I questioned her story about the black widow spider, but then she kept telling me about the other crawling insects. I told her to tell her landlord to have the exterminator come back. When Dale Hampshire refused and the problem persisted, I told her this was in violation of their contract. I recommended that if conditions got too bad and the landlord refused to correct them, she should move out. She said she didn't want to do that because she had a contract; however, when that huge spider scared her so, I guess she felt she had no alternative.

_____
                                                                        Affiant

SWORN TO AND SUBSCRIBED before me this _____ day of _____ ,

in the year _____ .

_____
NOTARY PUBLIC
State of _____
My Commission Expires:

Formulating Questions for Direct Examination and Cross-Examination

You may wish to use the following questions as guidelines to help the students prepare for direct examination and cross-examination. See the instructions on page 116 in the mock trial *Jack King and Jill Hamilton v. Harvey Miller* for more information.

The following example shows possible approaches by the plaintiff's attorney and the defendant's attorney to the same question.

Example: What was the real reason Clara Muffet moved out of her apartment?

Plaintiff: She realized she couldn't handle the financial obligation of renting an apartment.

Defense: The apartment was in an unlivable condition, and the landlord had not fulfilled his obligation to get rid of major insect infestation.

The following are examples of questions that might be used to help students explore the issues in the civil trial, *Dale Hampshire v. Clara Muffet*.

1. How accurate is Clara Muffet's description of the black widow spider?

2. How competent is Bugs-No-Moore?

3. Did Clara Muffet contribute to the spider problem?

4. How believable is Gale Johnston's testimony?

5. Do Clara Muffet's work habits have any bearing on her reaction to spiders?

6. How can Kit Smith's tolerance of spiders be compared with Clara Muffet's?

7. What is Dale Hampshire's responsibility as a landlord?

8. What documentation does Bugs-No-Moore offer for treating the apartment?

CAUTION: Remind the students that an attorney never asks a question on cross-examination unless he or she knows the answer the witness will give.

DALE HAMPSHIRE,
 Plaintiff,
-v-
CLARA MUFFET,
 Defendant

IN THE COUNTY COURT OF THE
THIRD JUDICIAL CIRCUIT, IN AND
FOR WEBSTER COUNTY, _____

CASE NO.: 98-88-CA

JURY BALLOT

V E R D I C T

Please circle your choice:

YES — Clara Muffet shall be held in violation of her lease and shall have to pay Dale Hampshire the sum of $3,500 for rent for the months of September, October, November, December, and January.

OR

NO — Clara Muffet shall not be held in violation of her lease.

DATED in Elms Grove, Webster County, _____ , this _____ day of _____ , in the year _____ .

_____
Foreperson

Lord Capulet
v.
Friar Laurence

Background Information

The last words of Escalus, prince of Verona, in Shakespeare's *Romeo and Juliet* lead the reader to believe that the feuding of the Capulets and Montagues was at an end.

We have looked at the play and asked, "What would have happened if this tragedy had happened in today's society?" Friar Laurence might have been regarded as a drug dealer or, at best, practicing medicine without a license. Certainly, the families might understandably be outraged that their children had been taken from them.

In our trial, Lord and Lady Capulet believe that Friar Laurence, the man who had meddled in their lives and, they feel, caused their daughter's death, must be brought to justice. The Capulets feel Friar Laurence, although a man of God, must be held accountable.

The Montague and Capulet families had been feuding for years. At the beginning of our story, Lord Capulet is hosting a masquerade party. On learning of the event, Romeo and his friends decide to crash the party. Romeo sees Juliet across the room, and it is love at first sight. Neither knows the other's identity. Even after finding out that they are members of the feuding families, the young lovers decide that they will not let the feud stand in the way of their happiness. Within 12 hours, they have arranged to be married by Friar Laurence, Romeo's spiritual advisor. Friar Laurence is not aware that Lord Capulet wishes his daughter, Juliet, to marry County Paris, a kinsman of the Prince.

Friar Laurence marries Romeo and Juliet, and the two leave, planning to meet again that evening. That afternoon, as he walks through Verona, Romeo comes upon a confrontation between the youths of the rival families. His friend, Mercutio, is accidentally killed by Tybalt, Juliet's cousin. Romeo, in turn kills Tybalt. As a result, Romeo is banished from Verona by Prince Escalus. After meeting with Juliet that evening, Romeo leaves for exile in Mantua.

To both Romeo and Juliet, banishment is worse than death. After Romeo leaves Verona, Friar Laurence, who has expertise working with herbs and medicine, offers a solution. Juliet will take a potion that will induce a death-like trance that will last for 42 hours. Her family, believing her dead, will place her in the family burial vault. Meanwhile, Friar Laurence will send a message to Romeo to take Juliet with him in exile.

Romeo does not receive the message, instead, Romeo's servant, Balthasar, who believes that Juliet has actually died, brings Romeo the sad news.

Romeo returns from exile to be with Juliet one last time. On his way back to Verona, he purchases a lethal potion with the intent of joining her in death. On entering the vault, he encounters County Paris, and in a struggle, Paris is killed. Romeo takes the poison, and, shortly after his death, Juliet awakens. Upon seeing her beloved Romeo dead, she takes his knife and kills herself.

The play ends with the burial of the young lovers and the two warring families at peace. Although the feud has ended, Lord Capulet has vowed that the individual who caused his daughter's death will be held responsible.

Because women had no legal rights at this time, Lord Capulet alone is suing in civil court, charging that by administering an experimental drug, Friar Laurence was directly responsible for the death of Juliet, Capulet's daughter. He also charges that by marrying Juliet Capulet and Romeo Montague without parental consent, the friar interfered in the completion of a contract that Lord Capulet had made with County Paris to marry Juliet.

For trial purposes, we have given exact dates for events even though Shakespeare only mentions specific days of the week. Because it is impossible to have principals in this play with names that are gender neutral, we have one female witness for the plaintiff and one female witness for the defense. You might want to consider using female attorneys to balance out the parts between males and females. Be careful to use as facts in the trial only those facts taken from affidavits, not from Shakespeare's play.

Definitions

Injunction - A writ granted by a court whereby one is required to do or refrain from doing a specific act.

Writ - A formal written document.

Exhibits

- The flask containing the potion that Juliet Capulet drank to induce the death-like trance
- Romeo's knife, which Juliet Capulet used to commit suicide

Note: Because the contract between Lord Capulet and Country Paris was an oral one, it cannot be used as evidence. It can be recognized as a legal agreement because there are persons who can vouch for the fact that the agreement was made.

Trial Participants

Plaintiff	*Defense*
Attorney(s)	Attorney(s)
Lord Capulet, Plaintiff	Friar Laurence, Defendant
Lady Capulet	Juliet's nurse
Escalus, Prince of Verona	Benvolio Montague

Pages 138 - 154 can be reproduced and used as beginning documents to present this mock trial.

DISTRICT COURT OF VERONA

LORD CAPULET,
  Plaintiff,

-v-

CASE NO.: 1414-CA

FRIAR LAURENCE,
  Defendant

STATEMENT OF FACTS

On Saturday, April 23, Lord and Lady Capulet hosted a masquerade party to which members of the most aristocratic families in Verona were invited. A notable exception was the Montague family, which had been feuding with the Capulets for generations.

Lord Capulet has stated that there was another reason for planning the party. He had invited County Paris, a kinsman of Escalus, the prince of Verona. Paris had asked Lord Capulet for his daughter Juliet's hand in marriage. Although reluctant at first because his daughter was only 14 years old, Lord Capulet said that if Juliet wished to be married to Paris, he would not oppose the union.

Young members of the Montague family attended the party without an invitation. It was there that Romeo Montague met Juliet Capulet. The couple was instantly attracted to one another—so much so that they vowed to marry as soon as possible.

Romeo arranged to have Friar Laurence, his spiritual advisor, perform the ceremony. Using Juliet's nurse as an intermediary, the marriage was planned for the very next afternoon.

After the wedding, Romeo left his bride, planning to meet with her that night. On his way home, he witnessed a confrontation between young Montagues and young Capulets. Words were exchanged, and before long, a fight broke out. Tybalt Capulet, Juliet's cousin, accidentally killed Mercutio, a friend of Romeo. Witnesses stated that Romeo pursued Tybalt, and in the ensuing duel, Romeo killed Tybalt.

Escalus, Prince of Verona, issued an order that Romeo was to be exiled to Mantua, never to return to Verona. At this point, a distraught Romeo visited Friar Laurence, seeking spiritual guidance. The friar counseled him to visit his new bride that night as planned and then to leave before daybreak for his exile in Mantua.

Lord and Lady Capulet stated that the following morning Juliet appeared very upset. They attributed this to Tybalt's death. Hoping to make his daughter happy, Capulet arranged for her to marry Paris the following Thursday after a suitable mourning period for Tybalt.

That same day, Paris visited Friar Laurence to arrange for his wedding to Juliet. While there, Juliet arrived. After a brief discussion, Paris left the friar and Juliet alone in the belief that she was there for confession.

Instead, Friar Laurence told her of a plan he had that would allow her to join Romeo in exile. The friar, who was known for his knowledge of medicinal herbs, had mixed a potion for her. She was to take it at bedtime on Wednesday, the day before her scheduled wedding to Paris. It would induce a deathlike trance that would last for 42 hours. Her family, believing her to be dead, would place her in the family burial vault. In the meantime, Friar Laurence would send a messenger to Romeo, telling him of the plan. Romeo would return and take the awakened Juliet with him into exile.

Juliet took the potion according to the instructions. The following morning, she appeared to be dead. The friar helped the family plan her funeral, and she was placed in the family burial vault. Meanwhile, due to unforeseen circumstances, Romeo never received the message from Friar Laurence. Instead, Romeo's servant, Balthasar, not knowing the truth, went to Romeo in Mantua and told him of Juliet's death.

On his way back to Verona to be with Juliet one last time, Romeo purchased a poisonous substance at an apothecary. He entered the crypt where Juliet lay. A grieving Paris had told friends he was going to visit Juliet's bier. When Romeo entered, a struggle apparently ensued, and Paris was killed. At this point, evidence points to a scenario in which Romeo committed suicide by drinking the poison he had purchased. It is believed that Juliet awakened to find both Romeo and Paris dead. She, too, then apparently committed suicide. Her body was found next to her husband's, her hand holding a knife she had used to stab herself.

When the Capulets and Montagues buried their children, Escalus presided over the ceremony. Both families vowed that the feud had ended.

Lord Capulet, however, has brought suit against Friar Laurence for the wrongful death of his daughter, Juliet. He also is charging the friar with interfering in the performance of a contract—the one he had made with Paris to marry Juliet Capulet.

He is asking for an injunction that would prevent Friar Laurence from ever again dispensing medicinal herbs. In addition, he would like the court to issue an injunction removing the authority that Friar Laurence has to perform marriage ceremonies.

DISTRICT COURT OF VERONA

LORD CAPULET,
  Plaintiff,
-v-
FRIAR LAURENCE,
  Defendant

CASE NO.: 1414-CA

GENERAL AFFIDAVIT

Lord Capulet , being first duly sworn according to law, deposes and says that:

Affiant

My family has lived in Verona for generations. We enjoy a comfortable life, and until the tragic death of our daughter, Juliet, we participated in many social gatherings. Unfortunately, our family and the Montagues had been at odds for years. No one really knows what started the feud, but it seems that each generation of young men perpetuated it. This was a definite contributing factor to the tragic events that led to the death of our only child, Juliet.

Less than a week before her death, we had no idea what tragedy was in store for us. I had arranged a large masquerade party and had invited members of all of the leading families in Verona—all except the Montagues, of course. Everyone of importance was there, including the Prince. It was on that fateful evening that Juliet first met Romeo Montague. I was not aware of this. That evening I was entertaining County Paris, a kinsman of Escalus, our prince. Paris had asked for Juliet's hand in marriage. I asked him to wait, as she was so young, but then relented and said that if she were willing, they could be married. He was to discuss the matter with her the night of the party. As it turned out, she had met Romeo and did not want to commit herself to marrying Paris.

The next day, the first of a series of unbelievably tragic events occurred. Our nephew, Tybalt, was killed in a fight with young Romeo.

When Tybalt died, Juliet appeared particularly distraught, and I decided that she and Paris should be married as soon as the three-day mourning period had ended. I had hoped the wedding would bring some measure of happiness into her life. When she was told of my decision, she became very upset, and I am afraid I lost my temper with her and told her the marriage must take place. Of course, I did not know at the time that she was already the bride of Romeo Montague.

When we discovered her dead the morning of her wedding day, it was with heavy hearts that we laid her to rest in the family vault.

The following day, we heard of the death of Romeo and Paris and were told that Juliet had stabbed herself. We learned the terrible truth—when we thought she was dead, she was really in a deathlike trance induced by a potion given to her by Friar Laurence.

Had it not been for Friar Laurence, our daughter would be alive today and married to County Paris, a kinsman of the Prince. The friar mixed his herbs and experimented on our daughter. He says he wanted to unite Romeo and Juliet in marriage because they loved each other, but the truth was that they had only met. He gave no thought to the fact that she was 14 years old and only a child. It was up to her parents to make such important decisions for her.

Friar Laurence said he hoped that the marriage would bring the Capulets and Montagues together. I must say he did succeed there, but at such a terrible price!

_____
                                          Affiant

SWORN TO AND SUBSCRIBED before me this _____ day of _____ ,
in the year _____ .

_____
NOTARY PUBLIC
State of _____
My Commission Expires:

DISTRICT COURT OF VERONA

LORD CAPULET,
  Plaintiff,

-v-

FRIAR LAURENCE,
  Defendant

CASE NO.: 1414-CA

GENERAL AFFIDAVIT

_____*Lady Capulet*_____ , being first duly sworn according to law, deposes and says that:

                    Affiant

   Juliet was my only child. I married young and gave birth to her at an early age. She received the best of care from a nurse who cared for her as if she were her own child.

   Lord Capulet and I enjoy a prominent position in the society of Verona and often host gatherings of the finest families. Unfortunately, due to a long-standing feud, we never associated with the Montagues. I never did understand this, but my husband decreed that no one in our family was to associate with them.

   Late in April, we hosted a masquerade party. Our parties had gained quite a reputation, and anyone of importance was there. I was especially pleased that County Paris, a kinsman of Prince Escalus, was in attendance. He had spoken to my husband of his love for Juliet and had asked for her hand in marriage. My lord said that she was just a child and too young to be married. I reminded him that when I was her age, I was already a mother. He finally agreed that if Juliet consented, he would allow Paris to take her for his wife.

   What had started out to be such a beautiful evening turned into a nightmare. Some of the young Montagues decided to attend our party even though they were not invited. It was there that Juliet met Romeo. Apparently, they fell in love. We had no idea how serious they were. Indeed, we weren't even aware they knew each other.

   The very next day, Romeo made arrangements for them to be married by Friar Laurence. I never understood why the friar agreed to do this. He knew that Juliet was so young, and he knew she did not have her parents' consent. Is not one of the Ten Commandments "Honor thy father and thy mother"?

That same fateful day, another tragedy occurred. Our dear nephew, Tybalt, was slain in a fight with Romeo. Tybalt had accidentally killed Romeo's friend Mercutio. Then Romeo sought revenge. Prince Escalus rightfully sought to regain peace and had Romeo banished to Mantua. When this all happened, we were not aware that Romeo and Juliet were husband and wife.

Juliet seemed especially upset, and we assumed that she was grieving for Tybalt. We had no idea she was distraught because her husband, Romeo, had been banished. My husband sought to make her happy and arranged for her to wed Paris the following Thursday. This timing allowed for a suitable mourning period for Tybalt. On the morning of what was to be her wedding day, we found her dead—at least we thought she was dead.

We went through the worst experience any parent could imagine. We planned our daughter's funeral and laid her to rest in the family crypt. Imagine our amazement when we were told less than two days later that Juliet, Romeo, and County Paris had all been found dead. Apparently Juliet had awakened from her drug-induced sleep and had stabbed herself after finding both Romeo and Paris dead.

To have to go through a second burial ritual is more than any parent should have to bear. Our daughter was taken from us twice.

Friar Laurence may be a man of God, but he has shown he has no compassion for his fellow human beings. Instead of acting as a mature guiding force and urging our children to wait, he agreed to marry them with just a few hours' notice. He cared nothing about the suitability of the match. Was Romeo the best husband for Juliet? Could he have provided her with the status that being the wife of County Paris would have given her?

I know the good friar has a reputation for his knowledge of medicinal herbs, but mixing a potion that would have such a strong effect—giving the user the appearance of death—was certainly irresponsible. He didn't even administer it but left it to a child to take by herself. Had she made a mistake, it would certainly have resulted in her actual death.

Come to think of it, it did do that, didn't it?

_____

Affiant

SWORN TO AND SUBSCRIBED before me this _____ day of _____ , in the year _____.

_____

NOTARY PUBLIC

State of _____

My Commission Expires:

DISTRICT COURT OF VERONA

LORD CAPULET,
  Plaintiff,

-v-

FRIAR LAURENCE,
  Defendant

CASE NO.: 1414-CA

GENERAL AFFIDAVIT

_____*Escalus, Prince of Verona*_____ , being first duly sworn according to law, deposes and says that:
       Affiant

    My family has ruled Verona for generations. It is a lovely place, and the people here are generally kind and peace-loving. The one exception has been the Montague and Capulet families. For as long as I can remember, the young men of these families have had regular violent encounters. I had instructed my guards to be aware of any trouble that appeared to be brewing and to step in and separate the offending parties immediately.

    On April 23, the Capulets hosted a magnificent masquerade party. I was pleased to hear that Lord Capulet was considering a possible marriage of his daughter, Juliet, to a kinsman of mine, County Paris. If Juliet agreed to the union, the marriage would take place soon. I thought it was rather unusual for a father to allow his daughter such freedom. Weddings joining important families are always arranged. That Juliet was to have a say in her future indicated that the Capulets did not have a tight rein on her behavior. This fact was eventually to prove tragic.

    The night of the party, I saw some individuals I believed to be Montagues attending. As everyone was wearing a mask, however, it was difficult to tell their identity. If they were Montagues, I was pleased because it indicated that perhaps Capulet had extended a friendly hand to an old enemy.

    The following day, I realized that peace was not to be. That day, the young men of both families fought. When it was over, two of them—one from each family—lay dead. Tybalt Capulet had killed Mercutio of the Montague clan. When Romeo Montague heard of the death, he sought out Tybalt. In the resulting battle, Tybalt was slain.

I knew Romeo and realized he was not the type of person to kill someone intentionally. Still, something had to be done to emphasize the severity of his actions and to let others know that such horrible deeds would not be tolerated. I decreed that Romeo was to be banished, never to return to Verona under penalty of death. At the time, I did not know that he and Juliet had married. Had I known, I probably would have given him a different punishment—what it would have been, I cannot say.

When I heard of Juliet's supposed death, I could only imagine the terrible grief her parents were enduring. Less than two days later, my guards came to me and told me the full extent of the tragedy. Three people had been found dead in the Capulet vault—Juliet, Romeo, and my dear kinsman, County Paris.

Only after interviewing Friar Laurence did I learn the details of this unimaginable calamity. As a man of God, I'm sure he had the best of intentions, but he showed exceedingly poor judgment. These were children, and he was treating them as adults. What right did he have to perform a ceremony that would bind them together for the rest of their lives? To make matters worse, he had used his knowledge of herbs to induce a highly dangerous deathlike trance. What right did he have to dispense such medications?

He says he thought that by marrying Romeo and Juliet, he would unite the two feuding families. Did he think he had more authority than I did to bring about such a truce? I had pleaded many times for peace between the two families. I will admit I was not as forceful as I could have been. Had I been, several of our finest young people would be alive today.

_____
                                                                Affiant

SWORN TO AND SUBSCRIBED before me this _____ day of _____ ,
in the year _____ .

_____
NOTARY PUBLIC
State of _____
My Commission Expires:

DISTRICT COURT OF VERONA

LORD CAPULET,
  Plaintiff,
-v-
FRIAR LAURENCE,
  Defendant

CASE NO.: 1414-CA

GENERAL AFFIDAVIT

_____*Friar Laurence*_____ , being first duly sworn according to law, deposes and says that:
      Affiant

    I am a member of the Franciscan order. Our order was founded by St. Francis, and we dedicate our lives to helping others. When I became a friar, I took an oath of poverty. St. Francis was very close to nature, and I dedicated a part of life to working with plants and herbs. I experimented with their medicinal qualities and how they could be helpful to others.

    I know most of the families in Verona and have been a confessor for many. I have had an excellent rapport with the young people. I was very close with Romeo Montague.

    Romeo often came to visit, and we talked about life in general. He was entering manhood and was eager to find a true love. He apparently was smitten with a young lady named Rosaline, and it was she he was hoping to see when he went uninvited to the Capulet party on April 23. Knowing Romeo, I do not believe he thought he was causing anything more than a bit of mischief by going to the party. He did not see Rosaline but instead was captivated by the lovely Juliet, daughter of the Capulets. The attraction was mutual and very intense. When he came to me afterwards, he told me that there would never be anyone for him but Juliet. He assured me that she felt the same way. I knew this young man since he was a tiny lad. With Rosaline, it was an infatuation; with Juliet, it was a real and abiding love. When he asked me to marry them, I hesitated but then realized that this was a union that must be given the Church's blessing. In addition, it would have the marvelous benefit of uniting two families who had been feuding far too long. It was bound to heal old wounds.

I performed the marriage ceremony. Shortly thereafter, the simmering feud between the two families escalated. Romeo's friend, Mercutio, was accidentally killed by Tybalt Capulet. In a second confrontation, Romeo and Tybalt fought, and Tybalt was fatally wounded. Our esteemed Prince had no alternative but to punish Romeo. Not wishing to sentence Romeo to death, he banished him from Verona forever. Should Romeo return, the death sentence would be enforced. The following day, Lord Capulet promised Juliet's hand in marriage to County Paris, hoping to help her overcome her grief over Tybalt's death. The date for Juliet's wedding to Paris was set for Thursday. Under no circumstances could I allow her to be married a second time.

Romeo and Juliet believed that Romeo's exile was a fate worse than death. I had to find some way to help them. I told Romeo to leave Verona and go to Mantua and that I would contact him. After he left, I remembered some experiments I had been doing with herbs. In my work with these plants, I discovered that they had some very unusual effects on the human body. A certain mixture slowed down the body to such an extent that, to the inexperienced eye, a person who had taken the drug would appear to be dead. After a little over a day and a half, the person would awaken and feel refreshed because of the deep sleep that had been experienced.

I felt I had no other choice than to offer this solution to Juliet. I had no idea what she might do. She repeatedly said that she could not live without Romeo, and I was afraid she might be suicidal. I also felt that once she and Romeo were reunited, their families would realize that these two young people were meant to be together and the family feud would come to an end.

After I had given Juliet the sleeping potion, I asked Friar John to go to Mantua and give Romeo a message from me. The message told Romeo what had happened and when he could come for Juliet. Unhappy fortune! Friar John went to find another friar to accompany him. This man had been visiting the home of someone with an infectious disease. Searchers were roaming through Verona sealing up homes of those believed to have such sicknesses. They came upon the two friars talking in one of these homes and sealed up the house so they could not leave. Friar John was never able to deliver the message and could not find anyone else who would.

When I found out what had happened, I went immediately to the tomb where Juliet was, knowing how frightened she would be if she awakened and found herself closed in a dead man's tomb. When I arrived, Juliet had just awakened. Both Romeo and Paris were dead. I heard someone coming and urged Juliet to follow me out of the burial vault. I did not find out until later that she had remained and, so distraught by her husband's death, had taken his knife and stabbed herself, joining Romeo in death.

General Affidavit continues on page 148.

As a man of God, I truly believe that He would not have shown me a way to help Romeo and Juliet unless I was meant to use it. God wants people to love one another, not to fight. I believe I was merely an instrument to carry out God's wishes. Fate dealt a terrible hand.

_____

Affiant

SWORN TO AND SUBSCRIBED before me this _____ day of _____ , in the year _____ .

_____

NOTARY PUBLIC
State of _____
My Commission Expires:

DISTRICT COURT OF VERONA

LORD CAPULET,
   Plaintiff,

-v-

                                      CASE NO.: 1414-CA

FRIAR LAURENCE,
   Defendant

GENERAL AFFIDAVIT

_____*Juliet's nurse*_____ , being first duly sworn according to law, deposes and says that:
    Affiant

    I have been in the employ of Lord and Lady Capulet since Juliet was a babe. I had lost my own dear daughter, Susan, shortly before Juliet was born. I always felt it was a blessing that God had sent Juliet to me to help ease the pain of my own child's death.

    I watched Juliet grow from a little girl to womanhood. I must say we were very close, and many was the time she would come to me with her problems. She really had trouble talking to her mother, Lady Capulet. I always felt Lady Capulet was more interested in the social happenings in Verona than in her own daughter.

    When I heard that County Paris had asked Lord Capulet for Juliet's hand, I was thrilled. Such a catch! My little girl was going to have a kinsman of Prince Escalus as a husband. Not only was County Paris from a fine family, he was very handsome, too.

    However, Juliet did not want to be rushed into marriage. At first, I thought it was because she was so young and frightened. Then I realized that she did not want to marry unless she married for love. The truth was, she didn't love County Paris.

    The night of the party, I saw young Romeo and his friends. I knew they shouldn't be there, but they seemed to mean no harm. I watched as Juliet and Romeo first met. I tell you, anyone could see it was love at first sight. The fact that Romeo was a Montague meant little to Juliet. She loved him for who he was. Although the Montagues and Capulets were lifelong enemies, she believed that this was an obstacle that true love would overcome. Romeo felt the same way.

    Romeo and Juliet knew their families would never agree to the marriage, so they asked Friar Laurence to marry them as soon as possible. You know how young love can be.

General Affidavit continues on page 150.

When the good Friar married them, he had no idea that Lord Capulet had arranged for Juliet to marry County Paris. When Juliet found out, she was very upset. She already had a husband. I knew I had to do something to help her. I thought that Romeo was as good as dead now that he had been exiled. He would never return to Verona to challenge Juliet's marriage to Paris. I wanted to help my dear Juliet, so I advised her to go through with the marriage. I told her that Paris was an eagle and that he was so quick and handsome. Why, I even called Romeo a "dishclout" and said he couldn't compare to Paris. I thought I had convinced her when she told me to tell Lady Capulet that she would wed Paris.

You can't imagine how awful I felt when, on the morning of what was supposed to be her wedding day, I found her in bed—not moving a bit. I thought she was dead. How could I have been so wrong? Maybe if I had looked closer, I would have seen some signs of life.

I don't blame Friar Laurence. He is a man of God, and he would never hurt anyone. He only wished for the young people to be happy and for the fighting between the Montagues and Capulets to stop. He had helped with the funerals of two young people from these families already, and he wanted no more of it.

I still can't believe my dear Juliet is gone. I feel as if I have lost another daughter.

_____

Affiant

SWORN TO AND SUBSCRIBED before me this _____ day of _____ , in the year _____ .

_____

NOTARY PUBLIC
State of _____
My Commission Expires:

DISTRICT COURT OF VERONA

LORD CAPULET,
　Plaintiff,
-v-
FRIAR LAURENCE,
　Defendant

CASE NO.: 1414-CA

GENERAL AFFIDAVIT

_____*Benvolio Montague*_____ , being first duly sworn according to law, deposes and says that:
　　　　Affiant

　　　　Romeo Montague was my dear cousin. We were more than cousins—he was my best friend.

　　　　On April 23, the morning of the Capulet party, I had an encounter with Tybalt Capulet, who was aching for a fight. I never understood his approach to things. Servants from the Capulet and Montague families were arguing and had their swords drawn. I tried to stop them, but instead of trying to settle the dispute, Tybalt made things worse. He said that he hated peace. If the Officers of the Peace had not come to stop the fighting, who knows what would have happened.

　　　　Afterwards, I spoke with my aunt and uncle, Romeo's parents. Lady Montague was worried about Romeo because she had not seen him all day. We saw him coming at a distance, and I told them I would talk to him.

　　　　When I spoke with him, it was obvious that he had become infatuated with the fair Rosaline. As we talked, some Capulet servants happened by and asked us to read a paper they had. It was a guest list for the party the Capulets were hosting that evening. Rosaline's name was on the list. I suggested that we go to the party even though we were not invited. It was a masquerade party, and we would have little trouble mingling with the other guests.

　　　　We became separated at the party. You know how it is when you are having a good time. After the party, Mercutio and I searched for Romeo. We thought that he must have made some arrangement to meet Rosaline secretly. We did not know about the fateful meeting between Romeo and Juliet. Mercutio and I left. I told Mercutio there was no use looking for someone who did not want to be found.

General Affidavit continues on page 152.

The next morning, we could not find Romeo and thought he must still be off somewhere, daydreaming about Rosaline. Even after we spoke with him, we did not know that he had fallen in love with Juliet. To make matters worse, Tybalt Capulet had issued a challenge to duel because Romeo had appeared uninvited at the party.

That afternoon was very hot, and tempers were also hot. I pleaded with Mercutio to go home because Capulets were about and looking for a fight. He refused, and soon the Capulets appeared. Tybalt and Mercutio exchanged words. About that time, Romeo appeared, and soon there was a real battle. Romeo tried to stop Mercutio from fighting and in doing so prevented Mercutio from defending himself. Tybalt's sword found its mark. Mercutio fell mortally wounded. After Mercutio died, Tybalt returned. In the battle between him and Romeo, Tybalt was slain.

Earlier in the day, Prince Escalus had warned that he would no longer tolerate fighting between the Montagues and Capulets. I told Romeo to leave immediately, for I did not know what would happen to him.

When the Prince came, I told him what had occurred—that Tybalt had begun the fight. He said he had no choice but to exile Romeo forever. The fighting must stop. I did not know at the time that Romeo and Juliet were husband and wife.

I have known Friar Laurence all my life. He is a good man. I am sure that his intentions were the purest when he married Romeo and Juliet. He wanted peace to reign in Verona, as I did.

Friar Laurence is also a very learned man, an expert with his herbs and medicines. Many of the families in Verona went to him for remedies to promote healing and relieve suffering. He rose early in the morning to harvest the herbs before the sun was fully risen. Juliet did awaken from the sleeping potion he gave her, just as he had predicted, so he did know what he was doing.

As for marrying Romeo and Juliet, the good Friar was a man who dealt with people on a regular basis. He knew human nature, and I'm sure he recognized that these were two very gentle people who were in love and should spend the rest of their lives together. Too bad that their time together was so short.

_____

Affiant

SWORN TO AND SUBSCRIBED before me this _____ day of _____ , in the year _____.

_____

NOTARY PUBLIC
State of _____
My Commission Expires:

Formulating Questions for Direct Examination and Cross-Examination

You may wish to use the following questions as guidelines to help the students prepare for direct examination and cross-examination. See the instructions on page 116 in the mock trial *Jack King and Jill Hamilton v. Harvey Miller* for more detailed information.

The following example gives possible approaches by the plaintiff's attorney and the defendant's attorney to the same question.

Example: Why wasn't Friar Laurence with Juliet when she awakened from the death-like trance induced by the sleeping potion he gave her?

Plaintiff: He was afraid someone might see him in the tomb and find out he had given her the medicinal herbs that made her appear to be dead.

Defense: He believed that Romeo would be there to take Juliet away and that it was unnecessary for him to be there.

The following are examples of questions that might be used to help students explore the issues in the civil trial, *Lord Capulet v. Friar Laurence*.

1. Why didn't Friar Laurence go to Lord Capulet when he was asked to marry Romeo and Juliet?

2. What would Lord Capulet have done if Friar Laurence had told him of the marriage plans?

3. Had Romeo and Juliet lived, would their marriage have healed the rift between their two families?

4. Are there other reasons why Lord Capulet is suing Friar Laurence besides the loss of his daughter?

5. Why has Prince Escalus agreed to testify if he is supposed to be a ruling authority?

6. How much responsibility must Prince Escalus assume for the deaths of Romeo, Juliet, and Paris?

7. Does Lady Capulet have other losses besides the death of her daughter?

8. Why is Juliet's nurse testifying on behalf of Friar Laurence and not her employer?

9. Why is Benvolio Montague testifying on behalf of Friar Laurence?

CAUTION: Remind the students that an attorney never asks a question on cross-examination unless he or she knows the answer the witness will give.

LORD CAPULET,
   Plaintiff,

-v-

FRIAR LAURENCE,
   Defendant

DISTRICT COURT OF VERONA

CASE NO.: 1414-CA

JURY BALLOT

V E R D I C T

Please circle your choice:

The court shall issue an injunction prohibiting Friar Laurence from dispensing medicinal herbs ever again.

   YES   NO

The court shall issue an injunction prohibiting Friar Laurence from performing marriage ceremonies ever again.

   YES   NO

DATED in Verona, _____ , this _____ day of _____ , in the year _____ .

_____
Foreperson

GLOSSARY OF LAW TERMS

Acquittal—The action taken by a trial jury in which it finds the accused not guilty and enters a verdict accordingly.

Affidavit—A written statement sworn to before an officer who has the authority to administer an oath.

Age of maturity—The age at which an individual shall be considered an adult; age 18.

Aggravated battery—A battery in which a person (1) intentionally or knowingly causes great bodily harm, permanent disability, or permanent disfigurement; or (2) uses a deadly weapon.

a.k.a.—An abbreviation meaning "also known as."

Appellate courts—Courts that review the record from lower courts for error.

Assumption of risk—The deliberate choice of an individual to risk a known danger.

Attractive nuisance—Something that is dangerous to children; attractive, alluring, or enticing to them; allows children themselves to create danger out of it; persons with such an object or condition on their premises owe a duty to protect children from such danger.

Bailiff—A minor officer of some U.S. courts who usually serves as a messenger or an usher.

Battery—An offensive touching or use of force on a person without the person's consent.

Civil trial—A trial involving a private dispute between individuals or corporations on such matters as responsibility for an accident, failure to fulfill the terms of a contract, malpractice, or damages from libel.

Closing statement—The final comments of an attorney reviewing points made during the trial and expressing conclusions.

Compensatory damages—Damages that equal the amount of loss and nothing more.

Contempt of court—Any willful disobedience to, or disregard of, a court order or any misconduct in the presence of a court; punishable by fine or imprisonment or both.

Contributory negligence—Occurs when an individual's conduct falls below the standard to which he or she is required to conform for his or her protection; the standard is that of a reasonable person under like circumstances.

Criminal mischief—An offense involving willfully and maliciously injuring or damaging by any means any real or personal property belonging to another, including, but not limited to, the placement of graffiti thereon or other acts of vandalism thereto.

Criminal trial—A court proceeding in which the case against individuals accused of breaking the law is presented.

Cross-examination—The examination of a witness by the opposing attorney to confirm or discredit the witness's testimony, knowledge, or credibility.

Defendant—The person defending or denying a charge brought against him or her; against whom relief or recovery is sought in action or suit; or the accused in criminal case.

Direct examination—The first examination of a witness by the attorney calling the witness.

Evidence—All facts, testimony, and documents presented for the purpose of proving or disproving a question under inquiry.

Exhibit—A document or material object produced and identified in court for use as evidence.

Felony—A serious crime, such as murder, larceny, or robbery, punishable by death or by imprisonment in a state or federal penitentiary.

First-degree murder—A homicide that is willful, premeditated, and deliberate.

Grand jury—At common law, a group of persons consisting of not fewer than 12 or more than 24 who listen to evidence and determine whether or not they should charge the accused with the commission of a crime by returning an indictment. The number of members on a grand jury varies by state.

Habeus corpus—An order signed by a judge directing a sheriff or other official, who has a person in his or her custody, to bring that person before the court to determine whether or not he or she should be released from custody.

Hearsay—That kind of evidence that is not entirely within the personal knowledge of the witness but is partly within the personal knowledge of another person.

Indictment—A formal written charge against a person that is presented by a grand jury to the court in which the jury has been sworn.

Inferior courts—Courts with limited jurisdiction. They fall under trial courts in the hierarchy of the court system.

Injunction—A writ granted by a court whereby one is required to do or to refrain from doing a specific act.

Insanity defense—A plea acknowledging the commission of the crime but asserting that there was no criminal intent because the defendant suffered from a defect of mind in which he or she did not understand the nature of the act or did not know that it was wrong; the defense is required to show that insanity prevented the requisite mens rea from being formed.

Judgment—The declaration, by a court, of the rights and duties of the parties to a lawsuit that has been submitted to it for decision.

Larceny—The illegal taking and carrying away of personal property belonging to another with the purpose of depriving the owner of its possession.

Lease—A contract by which one conveys real estate for a specified term for a specific rent.

Manslaughter—The unlawful killing of a human being without malice or premeditation.

Mens rea—Guilty mind; the state of mind required to be held criminally liable for an act.

Misdemeanor—A crime less serious than a felony that is punishable by fine or imprisonment in a city or county jail rather than in a penitentiary.

Murder—The unlawful killing of a person with malicious intent.

Notary public—An official authorized by the state to attest to or certify legal documents.

Opening statement—Statements made to the court to introduce the facts of a case.

Perjury—The offense of willfully making a false statement when one is under oath to tell the truth.

Petit theft (petty theft)—Larceny of things or goods whose value is below a statutorily set amount, which may vary by state.

Plaintiff—The party who complains or sues in a civil action and is so named on the record; a person who seeks remedial relief for an injury to rights.

Precedent—The body of judicial decisions in which were formulated the points of law arising in any case.

Preponderance of the evidence—Evidence that is of greater weight or more convincing than the evidence that is offered in opposition to it, or evidence that as a whole shows that the fact sought to be proved is more probable than not; with respect to the burden of proof in civil actions, it means evidence that is more credible and convincing to the mind.

Prosecution—A proceeding instituted and carried on by due course of law before a court for the purpose of determining the guilt or innocence of a person charged with a crime.

Punitive damages—Damages awarded by the court to punish a defendant, as for a serious wrong.

Reasonable doubt—Doubt based on reason and arising from evidence or lack of evidence; doubt that a reasonable man or woman might entertain and that can justify a verdict is not fanciful doubt, is not imagined doubt, and is not doubt that a juror might conjure up to avoid performing an unpleasant task or duty.

Security—Something given, deposited, or pledged to make certain the fulfillment of an obligation.

Self-defense—A legal defense that justifies the use of force against another to avoid personal injury or death; this defense is extended to defending others.

Subpoena—An order directed to an individual commanding him or her to appear in court on a certain day to testify in a pending lawsuit.

Superior court—A court of general jurisdiction intermediate between the inferior courts and higher appellate courts.

Treason—The offense of attempting by overt acts to overthrow the government of the state to which the offender owes allegiance or to kill or personally injure the head of state.

Trespass—In law, an unlawful intentional intrusion on another's property or person.

Verdict—The decision reached by a jury and reported to the court on matters lawfully submitted to them in the course of the trial of a case.

Witness—One who testifies in a court of law.

Writ—A formal written document.

Topic Index

All lessons in this book align to the following standards.

Grade Level	Common Core State Standards in ELA-Literacy
Grade 5	RI.5.1 Quote accurately from a text when explaining what the text says explicitly and when drawing inferences from the text. RI.5.3 Explain the relationships or interactions between two or more individuals, events, ideas, or concepts in a historical, scientific, or technical text based on specific information in the text. RI.5.6 Analyze multiple accounts of the same event or topic, noting important similarities and differences in the point of view they represent. RI.5.10 By the end of the year, read and comprehend informational texts, including history/social studies, science, and technical texts, at the high end of the grades 4–5 text complexity band independently and proficiently. RF.5.3 Know and apply grade-level phonics and word analysis skills in decoding words. RF.5.4 Read with sufficient accuracy and fluency to support comprehension. W.5.1 Write opinion pieces on topics or texts, supporting a point of view with reasons and information. W.5.2 Write informative/explanatory texts to examine a topic and convey ideas and information clearly. SL.5.1 Engage effectively in a range of collaborative discussions (one-on-one, in groups, and teacher-led) with diverse partners on grade 5 topics and texts, building on others' ideas and expressing their own clearly. SL.5.4 Report on a topic or text or present an opinion, sequencing ideas logically and using appropriate facts and relevant, descriptive details to support main ideas or themes; speak clearly at an understandable pace.
Grade 6	RI.6.1 Cite textual evidence to support analysis of what the text says explicitly as well as inferences drawn from the text. RI.6.8 Trace and evaluate the argument and specific claims in a text, distinguishing claims that are supported by reasons and evidence from claims that are not. RI.6.9 Compare and contrast one author's presentation of events with that of another (e.g., a memoir written by and a biography on the same person). RI.6.10 By the end of the year, read and comprehend literary nonfiction in the grades 6–8 text complexity band proficiently, with scaffolding as needed at the high end of the range. W.6.1 Write arguments to support claims with clear reasons and relevant evidence. W.6.4 Produce clear and coherent writing in which the development, organization, and style are appropriate to task, purpose, and audience. (Grade-specific expectations for writing types are defined in standards 1–3 above.) SL.6.1 Engage effectively in a range of collaborative discussions (one-on-one, in groups, and teacher-led) with diverse partners on grade 6 topics, texts, and issues, building on others' ideas and expressing their own clearly. SL.6.3 Delineate a speaker's argument and specific claims, distinguishing claims that are supported by reasons and evidence from claims that are not. SL.6.4 Present claims and findings, sequencing ideas logically and using pertinent descriptions, facts, and details to accentuate main ideas or themes; use appropriate eye contact, adequate volume, and clear pronunciation.
Grade 7	RI.7.1 Cite several pieces of textual evidence to support analysis of what the text says explicitly as well as inferences drawn from the text. RI.7.8 Trace and evaluate the argument and specific claims in a text, assessing whether the reasoning is sound and the evidence is relevant and sufficient to support the claims. RI.7.9 Analyze how two or more authors writing about the same topic shape their presentations of key information by emphasizing different evidence or advancing different interpretations of facts. RI.7.10 By the end of the year, read and comprehend literary nonfiction in the grades 6–8 text complexity band proficiently, with scaffolding as needed at the high end of the range. W.7.1 Write arguments to support claims with clear reasons and relevant evidence. W.7.4 Produce clear and coherent writing in which the development, organization, and style are appropriate to task, purpose, and audience. (Grade-specific expectations for writing types are defined in standards 1–3 above.) SL.7.1 Engage effectively in a range of collaborative discussions (one-on-one, in groups, and teacher-led) with diverse partners on grade 7 topics, texts, and issues, building on others' ideas and expressing their own clearly. SL.7.3 Delineate a speaker's argument and specific claims, evaluating the soundness of the reasoning and the relevance and sufficiency of the evidence. SL.7.4 Present claims and findings, emphasizing salient points in a focused, coherent manner with pertinent descriptions, facts, details, and examples; use appropriate eye contact, adequate volume, and clear pronunciation.

Common Core State Standards Alignment Sheet
Jury Trials in the Classroom

All lessons in this book align to the following standards.

Grade Level	Common Core State Standards in ELA-Literacy
Grade 8	RI.8.1 Cite the textual evidence that most strongly supports an analysis of what the text says explicitly as well as inferences drawn from the text. RI.8.8 Delineate and evaluate the argument and specific claims in a text, assessing whether the reasoning is sound and the evidence is relevant and sufficient; recognize when irrelevant evidence is introduced. RI.8.9 Analyze a case in which two or more texts provide conflicting information on the same topic and identify where the texts disagree on matters of fact or interpretation. RI.8.10 By the end of the year, read and comprehend literary nonfiction at the high end of the grades 6–8 text complexity band independently and proficiently. W.8.1 Write arguments to support claims with clear reasons and relevant evidence. W.8.4 Produce clear and coherent writing in which the development, organization, and style are appropriate to task, purpose, and audience. (Grade-specific expectations for writing types are defined in standards 1–3 above.) SL.8.1 Engage effectively in a range of collaborative discussions (one-on-one, in groups, and teacher-led) with diverse partners on grade 8 topics, texts, and issues, building on others' ideas and expressing their own clearly. SL.8.3 Delineate a speaker's argument and specific claims, evaluating the soundness of the reasoning and relevance and sufficiency of the evidence and identifying when irrelevant evidence is introduced. SL.8.4 Present claims and findings, emphasizing salient points in a focused, coherent manner with relevant evidence, sound valid reasoning, and well-chosen details; use appropriate eye contact, adequate volume, and clear pronunciation.
Grade 6-8	RH.6-8.3 Identify key steps in a text's description of a process related to history/social studies (e.g., how a bill becomes law, how interest rates are raised or lowered). RH.6-8.4 Determine the meaning of words and phrases as they are used in a text, including vocabulary specific to domains related to history/social studies. RH.6-8.6 Identify aspects of a text that reveal an author's point of view or purpose (e.g., loaded language, inclusion or avoidance of particular facts). RH.6-8.8 Distinguish among fact, opinion, and reasoned judgment in a text. WHST.6-8.3 Write narratives to develop real or imagined experiences or events using effective technique, relevant descriptive details, and well-structured event sequences. WHST.6-8.4 Produce clear and coherent writing in which the development, organization, and style are appropriate to task, purpose, and audience. (Grade-specific expectations for writing types are defined in standards 1–3 above.)